I SOLD MY HOUSE
IN A RAFFLE

A Proven Step-by-Step Method to Get Your Asking Price,
Save Money, Save Time, and Help a Charity Too!

Diane Giraudo McDermott

New York

I Sold My House In A Raffle

Cover Design by: 3 Dog Design
                  www.3dogdesign.net

ISBN 978-1-60037-731-0

Library of Congress Control Number: 2009939751

MORGAN · JAMES
THE ENTREPRENEURIAL PUBLISHER

Morgan James Publishing
1225 Franklin Ave., STE 325
Garden City, NY 11530-1693
Toll Free 800-485-4943
www.MorganJamesPublishing.com

In an effort to support local communities, raise awareness and funds, Morgan James Publishing donates one percent of all book sales for the life of each book to Habitat for Humanity. Get involved today, visit **www.HelpHabitatForHumanity.org**.

DEDICATION

A young Italian immigrant, age 18, paid the guy in the boiler room of a ship headed for America twenty dollars to hide him out. As the ship docked in New York, the young man jumped ship. He was immediately detained and put on the next ship leaving—the ship was destined for Africa.

After working in the diamond mines of Africa for over a year, the young man had saved enough money to return to Europe. Several years later, he finally found sponsorship for his passage to America. Although he arrived with only a few dollars in his pocket, he came armed with a wealth of determination. He worked in the steel mills of New York and Pittsburgh, the railroads in Arizona, and the shipyards in San Francisco. He went wherever there was work and was too proud to seek government assistance. At the time of his death, at age 82, he spoke five languages and had acquired land and a sizeable bank account to leave to his six children.

To my Italian grandfather, Michele Giraudo, who taught us by example that in order to reach your goals you must be resourceful and always be prepared to act in spite of the fear. Also, that if you sprinkle salt on a chicken's tail feathers you can catch the chicken—meaning, if you get that close to the chicken, then you can surely snatch it.

A Note from the Publisher

This book does not provide legal opinions or tax advice. It does not in any way replace the advice of counsel in assessing and minimizing legal risks in the sale of your home, in the holding of raffles, or in the tax ramifications of raffles. Professionals in your state familiar with these areas should be consulted before implementing the steps outlined. Specific states have restrictions associated with the holding of raffles, and the raffle holder is responsible for conforming to such restrictions. Sample materials provided in the appendices are for reference only and should be used only after consulting experts in the specific field to be sure they meet local and state laws and ordinances. Websites listed may no longer exist at the time of publication. The author and publisher specifically disclaim any liability for any misuse, or any damages arising from the use or application of the information in this book.

A Note from the Author

In this book you are instructed to sell raffle tickets on the Internet and across state lines. Yet some states do not allow selling raffle tickets on the Internet and others do—while some states have no definite answer on this issue. There are also differing opinions as to whether an organization can legally sell raffle tickets across state lines unless it is registered in every state. And there are a few states where raffles are illegal and prohibited

Some argue that the mandate is at the federal level dictated by the Federal Wire Wager Act of 1961—used to stop those engaged in online gaming, even though the law was designed for wire transmissions and passed prior to common use of the Internet. While others defend games of chance stating that the Act prohibits electronic transmission of information for sports betting across telecommunications. Others respond that the major concern of the United States Department of Justice is online money laundering.

You'll even find experts in the field of Internet law who disagree and some assert that the issue is answered at the state level. At the time of the writing of this book, nonprofits in 19 different states were conducting a house raffle—each of which were selling raffle tickets on the Internet and across state lines. House raffles in California were advertising their raffles on the Internet; but these California raffles did not accept ticket sales over the Internet due to a California statutory regulation.

My recommendation is that on the issue of selling raffle tickets online, and across state lines, is that each nonprofit organization should make its own decision with the help of an attorney who understands gaming and Internet law. I am not an attorney.

CONTENTS

LIST OF FIGURES

MY STORY

I was working two jobs in Oregon: teaching for a private school and selling advertising for a local magazine. In 2005, I left both jobs and returned to New Mexico to help take care of my mother who was diagnosed with cancer. After mom passed, I struggled to find work in Oregon, and I returned to New Mexico to invest in real estate.

After much looking, I purchased a four-bedroom fixer-upper and turned it into a beauty just as the real estate market took a downturn. Developers all around me were offering buyers incentives that I could not match, and buyers interested in my property could not qualify for a mortgage. At this same time, I was fostering three dogs that would otherwise have been euthanized by the city shelter. My prior marketing experience kicked in, and I knew I could sell my home in a raffle. I believed people would risk the cost of a ticket to win such a prize. However, just to be sure, I asked several people, and everyone I spoke to confirmed my belief. I began researching raffle regulations.

I partnered with a no-kill animal shelter who loved the idea. Within 45 days of the raffle start, I knew that the charity was struggling with the raffle. Ticket sales were slow, and, by virtue of the sluggish economy, the charity was weighed down by the fact that its donations were down by 62% while incoming animal rescues were up by 30%. Many homeowners facing foreclosure were making the difficult decision to surrender their pets. Some nearby shelters were closing their doors, and my charity was picking up the slack.

So I had a choice: let the raffle fail, or take charge. I took charge. I produced a TV commercial, placed advertising on radio, ran ads, created and distributed fliers, and held open houses. I even found businesses willing to sponsor some of the raffle advertising costs.

Due to the slow start, we had to extend the drawing date; but at the end I got my house sold for my asking price, and the charity made a chunk of money they would otherwise not have had. *I Sold My House in a Raffle* teaches home sellers and directors of nonprofit organizations that with diligent preparation they can fly out of the starting gate at lightning speed and get all those tickets sold and avoid the pitfalls. It will show the home seller how to partner with a charity that has the resources to get the job done, and how the home seller can be involved in the ticket sale process also.

INTRODUCTION

In a down economy, many home sellers face countless roadblocks from an overabundance of homes on the market, a drop in property values, to a large number of buyers unable to qualify for a mortgage. This same economic climate creates a significant drop in nonprofit charity donations from the public, reduced government spending for nonprofits, and an ever-increasing demand for services provided by these charities. As a result, home sellers are likely to experience months of struggle and frustration, and charities must cut back on their services or face closing their doors.

The purpose of this book is to partner homeowners with their favorite nonprofit charity to get their homes sold through a raffle with the home as the grand prize and thus provide a cash benefit to the nonprofit organization. The book is written for home sellers and fundraising directors of nonprofit organizations.

As a home seller, selling your house in a raffle is a way for you to get the fair market value, a below-market price, or a break-even price. The choice is yours—you are the seller. And you can enlist the services of a real estate agent and still use the house raffle process as a method to finding a charity buyer, or you can do this on your own without a real estate agent. The benefits of using an agent in a conventional sale of real estate are the same in a house raffle—the agent helps to find a buyer, the agent shows the property, and the agent walks you through the paperwork. However, although you may have the benefit of a realtor's expertise, it's critical that your agent has taken the time to learn the house raffle process.

This is a wonderful way for a nonprofit organization to raise funds, increase its data-base of donors, and create more visibility for its organization locally and nationally as well.

The greatest challenge all nonprofits face, in any economy, is raising money. So home sellers in an up economy may still take this opportunity to partner with a nonprofit organization offering their home as a grand prize and win on two counts—selling their home at the asking price without waiting for a qualified buyer, and supporting a worthy cause as well.

I Sold My House in a Raffle takes the home seller and the nonprofit director through the entire process—step-by-step. Home sellers must know precisely what it takes to have a successful raffle. This knowledge will help them during the interview process with different charities to be sure the charities understand the course of action and are fully prepared to get the required number of tickets sold. Secondly, a nonprofit organization might be very interested in holding a house raffle fundraiser, but may not know how to proceed, and having the raffle process outlined for them will show them the path to success. Thirdly, home sellers may find that they need or want to be actively involved with helping the nonprofit organization reach the target number of raffle ticket sales.

Understanding the Basics

Individuals cannot hold raffles because a raffle is a game of chance and considered to be a form of gambling. In most states, nonprofit organizations are allowed to hold raffles; therefore, the homeowner must connect with such an organization to raffle off their home. Throughout this book, the nonprofit organization is referred to as the charity.

▶ If you wish to skip the conventional process
of listing your home and waiting for a buyer, AND
you have always wanted to be "rich enough"
to help your favorite charity in a big way,
your time has come—enjoy!

Two Ways to Sell Your House in a Raffle

One way to sell your house in a raffle is where the charity purchases the home outright, and then holds a raffle with the home as the grand prize, and sells more tickets than the price of the home to ensure a profit for their organization. The charity might get a loan to pay for the home with an account set up at the lending institution where the raffle proceeds go as part of the security on the loan; or the charity may have the funds available to pay the purchase price or a part of it, and then pay the remainder at the conclusion of the drawing. If home sellers can find a charity that can utilize one of these options, they'll have a quick sale and they're done.

Another way to sell your house in a raffle is where the charity raises the funds through the sale of raffle tickets in order to pay for the home. This is the most common way, and this book provides a step-by-step process by which the home seller can get their asking price for their home and help a worthy cause as well.

Working With a Real Estate Agent

If your home is currently listed for sale with a real estate agent, and you wish to utilize the method of selling your house in a raffle, talk to your agent about contacting charities as possible buyers for your home. Selling to an individual and selling to a charity are very similar. In both cases, the agent will make a commission and the buyer will need to provide funding. The difference is that funding from a charity buyer may come at the conclusion of the raffle drawing after ticket sales are complete.

Your agent can keep the home active on the Multiple Listing Service (MLS) until a charity buyer is secured—not until the raffle drawing date, but until the charity signs a purchase agreement to buy. After that point, you have a pending sale and only back-up offers can be accepted. Your agent should verify that the Board of Realtors in your state has no restrictions on using this method to sell a home. Real estate agents might even consider contacting their expired listings with the idea of selling the home through a raffle.

Raffle Laws

Raffle laws vary by state. For example, according to the laws of Colorado, the organization must have been in existence for five years before an application for a bingo/raffle license can be made. Some states' raffle laws limit the number of raffles that a tax-exempt organization can hold in a year, and some require a special permit while others do not. Other states have specific laws about the value of prizes given away, the format of tickets, and other aspects of the raffle. Only a few states do not allow raffles, and some that don't are attempting to change that law.

> Before proceeding, check into the raffle laws for your state. Go to www.rafflefaq.com/united-states-raffle-laws and click on your state for the specific information about your state.

The first thing you want to verify is whether your state allows raffles. At the time of this publication, only three states did not allow raffles. If your state doesn't fall under the "no raffle law," then write down any restrictions your state imposes on raffles. This is a preliminary check, and the charity you partner with will be able to make a final determination of any restrictions.

Note: Purchasing a ticket for a charity raffle is not tax deductible. The IRS has declared that raffle purchases for valuable prizes are not tax-deductible contributions—the ticket buyer is purchasing a chance to win.

How to Read This Book

My recommendation, whether you are a home seller, a real estate agent representing the home seller, or the director of a nonprofit organization, is that you read this book twice. Read it first to learn how a house raffle works; then read it again taking action with each step. If you find that your state has specific elements for a house raffle, incorporate those elements into your raffle to avoid any problems.

The home seller and the charity must each know both sides of the raffle process. A charity does not want to partner with a home seller who doesn't have a good raffle house, and a home seller must partner with a charity that understands the process required to get the job done. When this is a good partnership, the results will be a win/win. So let's get started . . .

The Grand Prize

Y ou've probably heard the adage that for every home there is a buyer. That is, even a home with a strange floor plan and wild color schemes will appeal to someone either because it's exactly what that buyer is looking for as it is, or the buyer can see the potential in the home. Well, throw this theory out the window in a house raffle. Your home must appeal to not just one but to thousands of buyers in order to get the tickets sold. Your home has to charm the general public because few ticket buyers will risk even $100 if they don't like the prize.

So the first question is: Do you have a good raffle house? Review the following questions and decide if your home is a suitable grand prize.

Is My Home in a Desirable Area?

Here are some things that may be looked at as negatives:

- The home is on a busy street

- Neighbors have filled their yard with junk or old cars

- The home is next to an industrial building, a freeway, an apartment complex, or a bar

- Power lines run through the property and connect to a huge electrical transformer

- Homes in the area have not been maintained, and the neighborhood is deteriorating

- Nearby walls or fences have graffiti sprayed on them

Although you may be able to work out a solution with your messy neighbor and get the city to paint over the graffiti, other issues may be beyond your control.

Will My Home Appeal to the General Public?

A fixer-upper can still be a good raffle home if it is located in a prime location. For example, beachfront property may be a worthy prize even if the home requires some attention. However, it will be more difficult to get the tickets sold for a fixer-upper that is not in a prime location because many people are not comfortable with fixing up properties and would consider it a burden.

You may have a perfect raffle house if you just make a few changes. Take the time to evaluate your home and see if you can make some improvements so that it will appeal to the general public. Have you let the maintenance slide? Is the yard kept up? Do you need a new paint job? Without spending a lot of money, sometimes you need only a few minor adjustments to transform your home into a winner. There are a number of books on the subject of preparing your home for sale, and the internet is full of tips on this subject.

Is My Home Located in a Well-Populated Area?

Rural properties will be more difficult to raffle, and you need to have a substantial population to generate the number of ticket sales needed. Most people want to be near shopping, schools, public parks, and want to have easy access to the freeway. However, don't discount a mountain cabin because ticket buyers will like the idea of winning a vacation home.

▶ Rule of thumb:
25 people = 1 sold ticket

Can I Wait 6 Months to Sell My Home?

Ticket sales will take between 4-5 months. Then you have to consider time for the winner to claim the prize and go through the closing with the title or escrow company. Review your financial picture and be sure this will work for you.

How Do I Handle Encumbrances?

A mortgage, a second mortgage, and a home equity line of credit are all encumbrances, but they are not necessarily negative because the public views them as standard; most people realize that these loans will be paid off when the home sells. Because the charity receives title insurance at closing it has a free and clear grand prize to turn over to the raffle winner.

Negative encumbrances are things such as a contractor's lien, unpaid property taxes, or a property that's in foreclosure. If you have any of these encumbrances, don't lose heart, there's a way to handle all of them.

The first thing to understand is that when your home is the grand prize in a house raffle, it's in the spotlight, and potential ticket buyers may go online and investigate the public records. If they see liens and such, they may become frightened and not want to risk spending money to win a property with negative encumbrances, although these encumbrances can be paid off at the closing of the sale. So this is how you handle each of these:

Delinquent Property Taxes

Ask a family member or friend to help you pay off these late taxes—stress that in six months, at the conclusion of the raffle drawing, this loan can be paid back. You might sweeten the deal by offering a higher interest rate than the bank typically gives on savings accounts and certificates of deposit (CDs). Be cautious here because the raffle tickets must get sold to have a successful drawing, and none of the money is available until the raffle drawing is complete.

If there is no way you can pay off these past-due property taxes, then contact your County Treasurer's office (where you send your property tax payments) and find out your state's procedure for unpaid property taxes. For example, in the state of New Mexico, if you haven't paid your property taxes in three years, the state can auction the property. Find out the rules for your state first to be sure that during your raffle, the state doesn't schedule an auction of your home for unpaid property taxes.

If the drawing will be completed prior to a state auction, then be sure the equity in your home is enough to cover the back taxes as well as the mortgage and other debts associated with the property. At the time of closing, the back taxes and any late fees for this will be deducted out of your payment from the charity and be sent directly to the County Treasurer.

A Contractor's Lien

For the best interests of the raffle, it is your job to head off a disgruntled contractor. Contractors aren't happy when they have to file a lien against your property because they haven't been paid for their work. Again, see if you can borrow money and get the lien removed prior to the start of ticket sales. If this isn't possible, then inform the contractor that you have entered into a purchase agreement to sell the property to such-and-such charity, who is raffling the house, and that the full amount of the lien will be paid off at the time of closing.

Although contractors know their liens must be paid at the closing of any sale of the property in order to give the buyer title insurance (this is the purpose of the lien and constitutes the contractors' protection), notifying the contractor will help prevent the contractor from taking any negative action that might hurt your raffle. For example, in the middle of an Open House, the contractor might walk in and angrily announce that his company hasn't been paid for the new roof; or he might talk to a TV reporter, and before you know it, the story is on the evening news.

When the contractor understands that a house raffle means the house is being sold and a standard closing of sale will take place with a title company, the contractor will want you to succeed so that he/she can get paid. You may even find the contactor willing to participate in the raffle by purchasing a ticket. Use this same technique for other creditors with interest against the title to the property.

Bank Foreclosure

To foreclose, your lender will follow a judicial or a non-judicial process depending on the state in which your property is located. In any case, if you are behind in your mortgage payments or your lender has already sent you a notice of default, contact your lender stating that you have found a buyer for the property. Explain that a charity would like to purchase the home and raffle it off as the grand prize in its fundraiser. Ask the bank if it will extend you the time to complete the raffle drawing so that you can pay off the mortgage and fees.

This may also be a good time to see if the bank will reduce some of the late fees. Remember, banks are in the money business, not in the real estate business—they don't want to own houses. Foreclosing on your property will cost them money, so don't be hesitant to ask for this help. Also, don't think that contacting them will make the foreclosure process speed up and that maybe if you remain quiet it will just go away—it won't.

Finally, when you have negative encumbrances but have made the preceding arrangements, if anyone checks public records and finds these negative encumbrances, you can point out that the home will be delivered free and clear. Refer them to this notation from the Raffle Rules and Restrictions supplied in Appendix B which reads: ... *and all due property taxes, liens, and mortgages will be paid off at the time of closing, and the winner will receive a free and clear property covered by title insurance.*

If you were unable to push back the foreclosure clock and the bank will foreclose on the property prior to the raffle drawing date, then you cannot begin the raffle process. And before making a final decision to raffle a home, the charity buyer is protected from unforeseen encumbrances on the property because the title company will perform a title search and the charity has the opportunity to object to any title exceptions.

A Final Note Regarding the Grand Prize

While you can always improve on the condition of your home to make it more appealing, a poor location and other factors can be a downfall. Be realistic assessing your property. Do not proceed unless you feel comfortable that you have a good grand prize home, and that you are prepared to wait up to six months for the completed sale of your home.

If you're not sure that you have an appealing grand prize, then ask friends and co-workers to give you their opinions. Ask at least 10 people, "Would you risk $100 for a chance to win my house—if your odds of winning were (1 in 4,000) for example?" Then be open to accepting their responses.

Creating a
Winning Raffle Formula

Y ou're now working out the preliminary plan to get your house sold at your asking price on the date you choose.

The Home Sale Price

Obtain a thorough written market evaluation of your property from a well-known real estate agency in your area. You will rely on this evaluation, and the public will need to trust in this real estate agency as well. Take the mid-range comparable sale price, not the listing price, and calculate what you can realistically sell your house for and include the following.

- Closing costs at approximately $1,200 (closing costs will be low because this will be a cash buy with no lender involved). To get a better assessment of this cost, call the title or escrow company that you plan to use, and ask them. They will be happy to give you an approximate figure.

- Home Warranty at approximately $500. Check with a local home inspection company to get an exact cost for this. You want an inspection with a one year warranty.

- Six months of holding costs—approximately four to five months to get all the tickets sold and one month to close on the deal.

- Mortgage, property taxes, and other encumbrances on the property.

After making your calculations, be sure that your asking sale price to the charity falls within the range of comparable sales in your area.

The Home Sale Date

The actual closing date for the sale of your home will be after the successful completion of the raffle ticket sales and the drawing of the winning ticket(s).

▶ Hard economic times can make people
less willing to risk money on a raffle.
Yet, hard economic times can make people
more willing to risk money on a raffle
because winning would boost their finances.
So, in essence, any time is a good time
to hold a house raffle!

Yes, house raffles can work in just about any economic climate; but there are better times of the year than others to start selling tickets and to hold a drawing. For a number of reasons, the best month to start selling raffle tickets is May:

- The weather is good

- People have recovered from their holiday spending

- School is almost out

- Home buyers are out looking at properties

- People are anticipating their tax returns

February can be a slow month for ticket sales, while January, on the other hand, is the worst month to sell raffle tickets. People are feeling the bite from their holiday spending and are less likely to spend money on a chance to win. In addition, the weather isn't great, the real estate market is dormant, and people are focused on New Year's resolutions.

If you schedule a drawing on October 15 and you end up having to extend the drawing date for 60 days, then that puts you at December 14 for a drawing. This is still excellent timing. During the holidays the public is in a more giving spirit and would love to win a prize home for Christmas. So the main thing to remember when scheduling your raffle is to keep the month of January away from your raffle timeline. If this timing will not work, you can still proceed; but be aware of the effect the month of January will have on your ticket sales.

How Many Winners Do You Want?

The house is the grand prize; however, I recommend having a cash prize option as an alternative to the house and additional cash prizes as well. For example, the winner can take the prize home or $100,000 cash. I also recommend that you provide additional cash prizes for second place, third place and so on, totaling at least $5,000. Another option to extra cash prizes is donated merchandise from local businesses. At this point figure in the amount for additional cash prizes, and if the charity chooses to go with merchandise, you can make this adjustment to your figure later.

The reason you want to have a cash option as an alternate grand prize is that doing so will help sell tickets. Some people consider winning a house a burden because taxes are involved with winning a prize; therefore, taking the cash makes it simpler to pay those taxes.

Another reason for additional cash prizes beyond the grand prize is that it increases the ticket buyer's odds of winning, thus making it easier to sell tickets. Plus, on the day of the drawing, you will disappoint fewer people because you will have more winners—so less tissue to pass around.

Make the cash prize amounts at least double the ticket price so that people will have the chance of doubling their money. Tax ramifications are covered in a later step, but for tax reasons, you will want to keep each cash prize, except for the Grand Prize, under $5,000. Remember; you want to minimize the risk for ticket buyers because you want to get all the tickets sold. Take a look at the following example.

Grand Prize Winner:	Prize home or $100,000
First Place Winner:	$2,000
Second Place Winner:	$1,000
Third Place Winner:	$700
Fourth Place Winner:	$500
Fifth Place Winner:	$400
Sixth Place Winner:	$200
Seventh Place Winner:	$200

How Much Do the Tickets Cost?

I recommend setting raffle ticket prices at $50, $75, or $100 depending on the value of your property. If you have a high-end property worth over $1million, then you might want to increase the ticket price anywhere from $150 to $250. If you have to raise over a million dollars, it's better to increase the ticket price; otherwise, the total number of tickets will be very high and ticket buyers won't have good odds. People will risk $250 to win a home worth 1.5 million with only 8,000 or 10,000 tickets being sold.

Calculating the Number of Tickets to Sell

Raffling a house will be unlike other fund-raising efforts the charity has done where the dollar amount raised will be more or less the desired goal. In the case of a raffle, a required number of tickets must be sold. If not, the ticket buyers must be refunded their money if the drawing does not take place. In other words, in order to have a drawing, the charity will want to sell enough tickets to cover their costs (including the home purchase) and a profit for themselves.

Unlike the lottery, ticket buyers of a house raffle want to feel that they have a better-than-average chance of winning. In a lottery, the cash prize is usually so astronomical that people quickly forget that their odds of winning are slim. You need to give raffle ticket buyers good odds of winning, and to do so you must first calculate how many tickets you would need to sell to cover the following:

- Sale price of your home to include holding and closing costs, mortgages and other encumbrances, and still have a price which matches current comparable sale prices in your area

- Additional prize money

- Profit to the charity

Although ticket buyers may come from outside your state or area, you will sell most of the tickets to the local population. Some family members and friends will even pool their money to purchase tickets together. This is a good thing because it provides an opportunity for more people to be able to afford a ticket. It helps get the tickets sold faster.

As the drawing gets closer more tickets will be sold because ticket buyers will sense the urgency to act. They don't want to miss the chance to win.

▶ On average you'll sell
600-800 tickets per month.
More tickets will be sold in the last
two months than in the first two months.

There are, however, always exceptions. For instance, I heard about a house raffle that sold 4,000 tickets in 72 days, and another that took a year to sell 3,000. It all depends on thorough planning and strong marketing to publicize the raffle.

Consider the following questions when you create the best ticket sales formula for your raffle:

- How many tickets would give people good odds in comparison to the prize?

- What dollar amount can people in your area afford to risk on a raffle ticket?

- How motivated are people in your area to win the house?

- Considering the population of your area, realistically, how many tickets can be sold? You will want to broadcast your raffle nationally, but the majority of the ticket buyers will come from people who live in the area of the prize home.

Realize that the least amount of total tickets for sale, the better a person's odds of winning, and the easier it will be to sell tickets. However, if your grand prize is a million-dollar-plus home, you need to increase the number of tickets sold to reach your financial goal. Don't worry—people will still buy tickets because the prize is a higher value.

Let's assume you're selling 4,000 tickets at $100 each.

$400,000 Total ticket sales
- 250,000 Sale price of your home
-   5,000 Additional prize money to other cash winners
$145,000 Profit to the charity (not including expenses)

But what if the Grand Prize winner chooses cash instead of the house? The cash prize should be significantly less than the value of the prize home. This way, winners are motivated to take the home as their prize. However, should the winner take the cash, the charity can put the house on the market for less than the market price for a quick sale and reap a greater profit as shown in this next example.

$400,000 Total ticket sales
- 250,000 Sale price of your home
-   5,000 Additional prize money to other cash winners
$145,000
- 100,000 Cash prize to Grand Prize winner
$ 45,000
+175,000 Sale price of the home by the charity
$220,000 Profit to the charity (not including expenses)

A home with a fair market value of $250,000 should easily sell at $175,000, for example. This provides the charity a larger cash benefit, plus enough money to cover its expenses. You'll also find that by virtue of the added exposure of the prize home during the raffle, several people will express an interest in purchasing the house should they not win and the winner takes the cash.

Although the charity may reap a higher profit, it may not like the option of owning real estate. There is another alternative. The charity can pay the home seller an agreed upon price for keeping the property off the market for the duration of the raffle. Then the home seller can reduce the selling price of the home after the drawing for a quick sale. For example, the charity pays the home seller $50,000 after the grand prize winner chooses the cash option, then the home seller may reduce the sale price by $50,000 and still get their home sold.

If this type of arrangement is agreeable to the charity and the home seller, both parties should execute a written agreement to this effect prior to the start of the raffle. The charity would be obligated to pay the home seller the $50,000, for example, only if the raffle was successful, and only if the grand prize winner chooses the cash prize option. Be sure that your state does not have any restrictions in this regard.

Stop and Evaluate

N ow is the time to double-check if this process will work for you. A house raffle requires dedication, and you should not proceed unless you are committed to going all the way. The numbers can all be maneuvered according to your situation, so play around with different scenarios of ticket prices and number of tickets to come up with the best formula for your house raffle. Even though the charity is raffling off the home, you are the one who will present the best idea to them, and you will be assisting them in making the decision to offer your home as the grand prize in their fund-raising raffle.

You want to feel comfortable with the process so that when you pitch your idea to the charity staff or board they will see that they have partnered with someone who has done the necessary research and understands the risks involved and the course of action required.

Take the time now to evaluate your personal situation and your intentions honestly. If you are merely looking to get your house sold and there is no desire to help a worthy cause, then the element of greed will get in your way. Write down your answers to the following questions. Saying the answers to yourself is not enough. Putting your answers down on paper requires a commitment to the responses—you'll see.

- Have I realistically calculated my finances to know that I can hold my home for the required time to get the tickets sold?

- Is offering my home as a grand prize in a house raffle the best way for me to get my property sold? Why?

- Have I always wanted to help a charity in a big way? Why?

- Does selling my house by partnering with a charity sound like it would be interesting and fun to do? Explain.

- How would I feel if the tickets are not all sold and the raffle is canceled? If I still own my house will my finances be adversely affected? Will I be okay?

So you were honest with yourself, and you remain confident that selling your house in a raffle is a good solution for you; I congratulate you on the beginning of a unique and rewarding adventure. Go for it!!

Searching For the
Right Charity

I n the United States, nonprofit organizations are created by incorporating in the state in which they expect to do business. The act of incorporating creates a legal entity enabling the organization to be treated as a corporation. The main difference between a nonprofit and a for-profit organization is that a nonprofit does not allocate excess finances or resources to owners or shareholders. Although the nonprofit can have employees and even compensate directors, excess finances and resources are used to help pursue its goals, and most nonprofits have a large percentage of their staff as unpaid volunteers.

According to the National Center for Charitable Statistics (NCCS) currently there are over 1.5 million nonprofit organizations in the United States. Over 62 million Americans volunteer and the growth rate of Americans working at a nonprofit organization in the last 25 years is 50%.

Six Possible Charities

Make a list of at least six charities with whom you would like to partner on your house raffle. What you're looking for is a 501(c) tax-exempt organization because most states require that an organization be recognized by the IRS as exempt from federal income tax before issuing a license to conduct charitable gaming. If you're not familiar with the charities in your area, then do an internet search for nonprofit organizations in your city or state.

The office of the Attorney General oversees charities (except for religious and educational organizations). This office has an obligation to protect the public and to investigate whether the charity's assets are being used for its intended charitable purposes. Check your state attorney general's website as it may include a list of charities that exist in their jurisdiction that you can use for your search.

You will want to include six charities on your list because some may not be workable. For example, some charities may not want to try a house raffle fund-raising project or the timing isn't right for them. Then there are those you may eliminate because they don't fit your criteria. You're looking for likeable and strong charities.

Likeable Charities

Choose organizations you like, those whose cause you believe in. For instance, the charity I chose had been in the area for over 12 years and it rescues over 5,000 animals each year. The charity had a well-deserved positive reputation, and many local residents had adopted pets from this charity so they were motivated to help.

When considering the charities for your list, local organizations are better for a house raffle than national charities. The public is more apt to want to help a local organization than a national one with whom they may not be familiar. Ticket buyers view helping a local organization as having a direct impact on their own lives; but if there are no suitable local charities, then try to choose a local branch of a national charity.

> ► Primarily, people buy raffle tickets
> for a chance to win.
> Secondarily, people will risk *not winning*
> in order to help the charity.

You want your charity to be "support worthy." In other words, will the public view this charity's cause worthy of their support? Will the public consider the charity's cause worth their hard-earned money? The cause may be very important to the founders of the organization, but does it serve a universal need with which the general public can connect? Children, pets, human diseases, the planet, endangered species, veterans, the poor and the homeless are just some examples that touch people's hearts. In your search you may find many other great causes that have a universal appeal.

If the charity has a website, read about it there. Then go to the online website of your local newspaper and television stations and search for any past stories about the charity. If your charity is in the news with positive stories, then this is a good sign. For later reference, take notes as you research these charities.

Strong Charities

Look for charities that have the manpower and resources to handle the undertaking of a house raffle. It requires organization and determination to manage a house raffle and to sell thousands of tickets. New charities in existence for less than 3 years will probably have fewer resources to spare working on the raffle. Later on, when you meet with the charity, you will need to find out if the charity has an active Board of Directors who will help with the raffle, whether they have media connections and a large donor list, and whether they have a strong track record of knowing how to raise money. Take a look at the charity's upcoming fundraising events and see if they have a pool of strong sponsors listed for the event. Sponsor names will be noted on the advertising for the event.

Public and some private schools are often good nonprofit organizations to handle a house raffle. A positive to consider about schools is that they have a built-in sales force of hundreds of students who can sell tickets to family and friends. Since the profits from the raffle will directly help these students, their parents and the public will be eager to support the raffle. Consider the athletic booster club of the high school in the district in which your prize home is located, or check out your old alma mater if it's located in a neighboring city.

At this early stage, you may not be sure if the organizations on your list can handle a house raffle. Remember, you are only making assumptions; and as you gain more information about the groups, you will be able to verify your assumptions before you sign on with any organization.

Which Charity Is Best?

Now that you have a list of six charities, prioritize the list by rating each charity using the criteria provided. Right now your rating will be an educated guess based on your research information. After you meet with the charity, you can reassess your answers for a more accurate evaluation.

Make six copies of the following chart and rate each charity on a scale of 1-10 (1 being Low, and 10 being High)

Rating	Charity Years in Existence _____
	How passionate am I about this charity's cause?
	How well known is this charity by the local public?
	How well liked is this charity by the local public?
	How much direct impact does their work have locally?
	How positive was the media about this charity?
	How much does the public consider them worthy of support?
	How universal is their cause?
	How strong are their financial resources?
	How strong is their manpower to handle a house raffle?
	How active is their Board of Directors?
	How much do I know about this charity?

Add the total for each form. You're going after the charities that rank the highest first. Keep these charts for reference. You may find your answers changing as you begin meeting the directors and staff at the charities.

If you found that your rating to the last question was below 5, then try to obtain more information on this charity so that you have enough data to adequately consider them for your house raffle. You might take a look at Charity Navigator – Your Guide to Intelligent Giving. Their website is www.charitynavigator.org. On Navigator's website focus on these categories:

- 10 Most commented charities
- 10 Least reviewed charities with high ratings
- 10 Highly-rated charities with low paid CEOs
- 10 Charities drowning in administrative costs
- 10 of the best charities everyone's ever heard of
- 10 Highly rated charities relying on private contributors
- 10 Charities routinely in the red
- 10 Charities expanding in a hurry
- 10 Charities in deep financial trouble

Consider replacing the limited-information charity on your list with a charity on Charity Navigator's list. It is best if the charity has a local branch; and be careful not to automatically discount charities with financial difficulties because the charity could still pull off a house raffle if it had *adequate manpower.*

Meeting With the Charity

N ow you're ready to contact the director of the first organization and schedule an appointment to meet. Then you'll be ready to organize your thoughts and the materials needed for the first meeting.

Making the Phone Call

Even if you have never contributed financially to this charity, part of the reason you chose it is that you believe in their cause—so you are a supporter. Make the phone call and explain that you are a supporter of their cause, and you would like to speak to the person in charge of fundraising.

You might reach a receptionist or assistant who asks, "May I say what this is regarding?" Don't be afraid to "spill the beans," you've got a good thing here. Respond that you would like to offer your home as a prize in a fundraiser to benefit their organization with approximately $_____." Since this figure is not solid yet, state a profit amount slightly under the figure you created in your ticket sales formula. This will get the assistant's attention and they will want to push your call through to the decision-maker.

Most charities will be interested to listen. One exception is that there are some religious groups that consider a raffle to be morally wrong; so if you reach one of them, just thank them for their time and go to the next charity on your priority list. Refrain from the temptation to get into a debate about morality. Your goal is to find a charity that is excited about your idea, not one you have to convince.

Wrapping Up the Call

If the decision-maker is not available, ask to leave that person a message. Find out the name of the person you're speaking with and get the name of the decision-maker. Keep a record of dates and times. If they don't respond in about 4 days, call again to inquire. Sometimes a charity is interested, but it is inundated with the day-to-day operations. Many times the director does this work for no pay, so your persistence here will benefit both of you.

It may also take some researching and additional calling to finally connect with the actual person or persons who can make the decision for the charity. A house raffle may need approval by more than one individual or an entire Board of Directors. If you are serious about raffling your home, don't give up at this point. It can be a frustrating step; but there are charities that would *love* to have this opportunity, so you just need to keep moving forward.

Once you speak to the director of fundraising, then set up a time to meet so that you can completely explain the house raffle process. Try not to give too much information over the phone—you want the opportunity to meet face-to-face so that you can also evaluate the charity, and walk them through the benefits of a house raffle.

Organizing the Meeting Details

Find out how many people will be at the meeting. Bring enough copies plus a few extras of the following:

- A cover page titled Raffle in Support of _____.
  (Name of charity)

  Put your name and contact information at the bottom.

- Basics of a House Raffle (see Appendix A).

- Typed examples of your ticket sales formula when the winner chooses the house and when the winner chooses the cash prize option.

- Copies of the Raffle Rules and Restrictions (see Appendix B).

- Photographs of the house—inside and out.

- Typed information about the house to include the following:

  o Square footage
  o Lot size
  o Age of the home
  o Type of heating and cooling
  o School district
  o Value of the home

- Copies of the fair-market property evaluation that you obtained from a real estate agent.

Review your research notes regarding the charity you plan to meet with so that you can be prepared to speak to them about their organization. Make a list of any questions you would like to get answered about the organization and its ability to promote ticket sales for the house raffle. Review the marketing promotional ideas listed in STEP 7 as this will help you get an idea of the things you can suggest to the charity.

At the Meeting

At the first meeting you need to put the charity's decision-makers at ease and answer any questions that may arise while you also get your questions answered in order to evaluate the charity adequately. Consider this similar to a job interview except that both parties are interviewing for the job. If the charity's decision-makers recognize the benefits of a house raffle and if they like you and your home, they will want you to partner with them; and vice versa, if you like the charity, you will want them to accept your house for the raffle.

Setting the Stage

First let everyone know why you picked this particular organization and how the charity will benefit from doing the house raffle. Explain your belief in their cause. For example, do you have a life story you can share that made you appreciate the charity's work? Let the group know you did your homework, and you know more about the charity than just its name.

Allow the charity's representatives to tell you more about their organization; you might ask them some questions regarding information you read on their website or about how they initially got started. Also, tell them about you and your home. They may like to hear about your career, and the reason you want to sell the home.

Benefits to the Charity

Remember that there are two additional benefits for the charity beyond the monetary profit: an added number of contacts in its database created from ticket buyers and the added exposure for the charity.

Be open to altering the numbers in your ticket sales formula to fit the charity's needs. Just be sure the changes don't veer too severely from the criteria for a successful raffle and that you are still getting the price you need for your home.

If the charity is interested, but insists on reducing the sale price of the home to increase their net profit or reduce the number of tickets to sell, then you must help your charity members to gain a better understanding of the foundation of a house raffle. Since this is not a conventional sale of real estate where the sale price is negotiated and the buyer (the charity) can close on the sale in 30 to 45 days, negotiating of the home sale price doesn't usually work in a raffle. In a raffle, the homeowner must wait for the tickets to get sold and also risk that the tickets might not get sold. So the only benefit to the homeowner is that they get their property sold at their asking price, which of course, must be firmly based on comparable sold properties in the area. So if this becomes an issue with your charity, then review the benefits to both parties for better clarification. A house raffle must be a win for everyone.

Reviewing Your Handouts

Go through your handouts, starting with the basics of a House Raffle. Ask whether the charity is aware of any state restrictions that may apply and then review any that you found in the raffle laws for your state. The charity may be well aware of raffle restrictions that apply to its organization, because a major element of its operations is fundraising. The office of the attorney general in your state may also provide guidelines.

Resources to Succeed

Ask if they have the resources to promote the raffle. Since nonprofits have regular donors, they have ways of getting the word out by monthly newsletters, e-mail, and earned media. Ask how many people are on the donor list and whether it is up to date. The charity may be able to connect with businesses interested in sponsoring commercials for TV or radio and print media as well. Find out if they have an active Board of Directors that would be willing to help. Some nonprofits have Board members who are very influential people with great connections in the community.

Marketing Considerations

Discuss any promotional marketing ideas the charity may have in mind to promote the house raffle. For instance, does the charity have an advertising agency that provides services to the organization? Can the charity create a website for ticket buyers to see photos of the prize home, read the Rules and Restrictions, and provide a place for secure online credit card purchases? Adding this information to their current website is not as effective because viewers become side-tracked by other items showcased on the charity's general website. You want a website dedicated to the house raffle.

Although a house raffle is out of the ordinary, charities are accustomed to holding fundraisers. They should take a realistic view as to whether they can successfully handle a house raffle. Be careful to watch for clues as to whether they are biting off more than they can chew: "Piece of cake, we can sell 4000 tickets!" It's never a piece of cake when you're dealing with the public, so take this as a gigantic red flag. And marketing the raffle must go beyond sending a letter to current donors.

▶ Rule of thumb:
$1,000 in advertising = 300 ticket sales
Yet, media interviews and newspaper stories
which are both *free*, will bring in more
ticket sales than paid advertising.

Ask the charity's representatives to tell you about other fundraisers they've done that required a similar number of responses. Find out if they have volunteers that could assist with promoting the house raffle or selling tickets. Find out as much information as possible about how the charity would go about getting the tickets sold.

If you are in a position to help with ticket sales, or if you have a sales or marketing background, then this is the time to step in. Another consideration is to assist with the advertising costs. If possible, for instance, you might offer to sponsor a radio commercial for $1,000. Remember, if you were to sell your home in the conventional way chances are you would not get your asking price, so this is little cost to get your home sold. However, don't just blindly offer $1,000—offer it towards a specific media. I chose radio because you can get a large number of 15 second spots for $1,000, and because it is a nonprofit, the radio network will provide a Public Service Announcement (PSA) reel which means that the station will provide a match to the paid spots thus making your advertising dollars go further. The charity can choose the station that best reflects its demographics.

Your donation for this advertising will show your commitment to the plan. If necessary, you can always account for this in the sale price of the home. The only risk to you is that if not enough tickets are sold for a successful raffle and the drawing is canceled, then your money spent on advertising will be a loss—or you could call it an investment in a good cause.

▶ If you carefully follow the steps I've outlined,
and pick a charity that meets the raffle criteria,
your chances of success will multiply ten-fold.

Closing the Meeting

If the nonprofit is definitely interested, ask those involved to draft a preliminary marketing plan to present to you so that you can feel comfortable that the raffle will be a success. Explain the risk you are willing to take for the raffle. You will be taking your home off the market for approximately 6 months, but still continuing to pay mortgage, taxes, insurance, and utilities. If the raffle doesn't succeed it would be a financial detriment to you.

If all looks favorable, schedule a second meeting date in approximately 10 days. Give your charity time to consider the ramifications of a house raffle, come up with additional questions, and time to draft a marketing plan to sell the number of required tickets. Don't expect to meet with the charity and start selling raffle tickets the following week. The marketing plan is crucial and must be in place before the raffle starts.

The second meeting should take place at the prize home or set-up a time for the charity's decision-makers to view the home prior to the next meeting. The charity is the buyer of your home, and those involved must be comfortable with their purchase.

> ► If the charity is hesitant,
> don't try and talk them into it—you
> want a committed partner.

Double-Checking

After the meeting, review the ratings you gave this charity on your rating sheet to be sure you're still on target. In the event that the first meeting proved that this charity is not the right one because it cannot handle a house raffle or the organization has decided not to take on this project, then call the second charity on your list.

Hey Everybody,
There's a Raffle!

T his step explains how to promote the house raffle. Review the ideas presented and expenditures necessary to advertise the raffle to the public effectively. Your charity will organize and manage the marketing of this fundraiser; but as the home seller, you need to be familiar with this information too. You might be able to help them.

The charity can choose the ideas that best fit the organization, modify them to fit, or use ideas of their own. In any event, a complete marketing plan must be in place prior to selling the first ticket. Getting all the tickets sold is a race to the drawing date and you want to leave the starting gate at top speed.

Although I recommend that the charity not sell raffle tickets to residents of states that prohibit raffles, the charity will want to broadcast the raffle outside of your local community because you want as many people as possible to consider purchasing tickets. Remember that the winner doesn't have to move into the home—it may become an investment property, a second home, a home given to grandchildren, or a home quickly sold at a below-market price to make money fast. And don't forget to take into account that the winner can choose the cash prize instead of the home.

▶ With over 300 million people
in the United States,
use this to your advantage
and let everybody know
about your house raffle!

Marketing Expenses

Many promotional ideas take time and effort but little money, while others will require more cash. One way to offset expenses is to ask local business to sponsor the raffle. These businesses will have their names printed on your fliers, tickets, ads, and their name can be mentioned on radio or TV advertising and interviews. This is a win-win situation for everyone. Businesses get added exposure and the sponsorship money will increase your chances of success. You'll be surprised how many businesses will respond positively to a sponsorship request.

Marketing Options

Look at the following ideas for the best ways to promote the raffle. Add your own ingenuity and imagination to create lively and attention-grabbing materials. Seek national recognition; and remember that television and radio interviews as well as newspaper stories, which are all free, will bring in more ticket sales than paid commercials. The charity should take advantage of these free avenues to get the news of its raffle out to the public, and the message of how the raffle proceeds will help the charity's cause.

Print Media

Fliers

The flier should include the web address in case ticket purchasers want to buy online, and it should have the Entry Form on the backside so they can easily Fax or mail it in with payment. We printed two fliers, a general flier, and an Open House flier. Take a look at the sample fliers in Appendices K and L.

Printing can be free or at a discount by including "sponsored by _____" on the flier and having one of your sponsors pay for it. If you do an 8.5" x 11" one-sided flier, you could allow up to four businesses to advertise on the backside for a charge that covers the cost of the fliers. Always use all the digits in your cash award amount—print $100,000.00 instead of $100,000 or $100K. It's the same amount, but which one looks like more?

Fliers can also be created to fit on a half page vertical with the Entry Form on the back. Avoid creating half page horizontal fliers as they have less visibility than a half page vertical, especially if they're inserted into newspapers.

▶ Rule of thumb:
50,000 fliers = 1500 ticket sales

After the fliers are printed, charity volunteers can canvas local businesses to insert the fliers into customer bags. Businesses should do this at no cost. Grocery stores are excellent for this as they get approximately 7,000 customers per week. The charity volunteer should ask for the store manager, show the manager the flier, and explain how the house raffle will help the charity. In my experience, 8 out of 10 grocery store managers agreed to stuff our fliers into their customer bags. Hint: If you call the store's corporate office, they'll tell you it's against company policy; but if you just walk in and ask the store manager, you'll probably get a "yes."

Don't forget to canvas designer coffee stores, bookstores, video stores, pizza, ice-cream shops, and gas stations with convenience stores. Contact partner businesses too. A partner business is one that shares a connection to the charity. For example, a store that sells pet supplies is a partner to an animal shelter. A breast-imaging center is a partner to The Breast Cancer Foundation. Ask the partner businesses if they would place fliers on their counters or insert them into their customers' bags.

In the city where my house was raffled, we have a service that delivers to resident's driveways a plastic bag filled with fliers. The fee for this service is reasonable at $30 for 1,000 fliers. Your flier will be among many in the bag, but residents usually thumb through the fliers in the bag and keep the ones that appeal to them. In our case, this was a donated service to the charity. You might check into this type of operation available in your area. The charity can also use direct mail service companies or bulk-mail pricing for nonprofits through the U.S. postal service.

Posters

Create large posters and place them throughout the community and at every event the charity hosts. Make sure they are at raffle ticket purchase sites too. Some businesses will not agree to hand out your fliers to their customers, but they won't mind a poster in their window.

Newsletter and Mailings to Supporters

Prominently advertise the house raffle in any newsletter being sent before the drawing date. If resources allow, send a letter to prior contributors. Emphasize the charity's past good work and how beneficial a successful raffle will be.

Press Releases

There is no charge to send out a press release. Once the press release is received by the media, they can choose to print or broadcast the information depending on their interest and scheduling needs. Create a strong heading and keep it to 4-5 paragraphs outlining your top points on one page with lots of white space—and accuracy is critical. Include your contact information in case they have a question and include the words, "For Immediate Release," in bold type.

Make sure your media list is up-to-date so that you are directing your press release to the right person. Usually the editor or assignment editor and the reporter on your beat is the person you want to receive your press release. Send it to newspapers, TV, and radio stations. The best way to send it is by e-mail and follow-up with a mail letter and telephone call. If the charity works with an advertising agency, the agency will have the ability to send the press release to all the right spots.

It's important to get credibility quickly in order for the public to support the house raffle. After a local news anchor mentions the house raffle on TV or radio, local businesses will suddenly be interested in becoming part of the event as well. These businesses may even sponsor a TV or radio commercial. If you can locate a national reporter who could follow your story, this can skyrocket your ticket sales.

Newspaper Advertising

This advertising includes line-ads, display ads, and flier inserts. Display advertising contains text plus images such as logos or photographs. With display advertising you can center text and use different size fonts. In periodicals, display advertising can appear along with general editorial content. In contrast, classified advertising is usually in a distinct section with text only. Lead-time for display ads is longer than for classified.

You'll have greater impact by inserting fliers into the newspaper than to run a display or a classified ad. Try to get these fliers printed for free or at a discount. It's important not to ignore the smaller papers in your area. They will have a strong readership base, and your inserted flier will have good visibility. Also, check if the newspaper has a "wrap" that holds the fliers. Many times the advertising space on the wrap is offered to nonprofits at no charge. Remember to contact newspapers in other states as well.

Newspaper Stories

These should be at no cost. Do as many as possible. If your charity has a special event happening, get it mentioned in the paper along with information about the raffle.

Billboards

Always ask for donated space, and keep your message simple, for example:

Win a House
Only $100   *Photo of the house*

Benefiting AAA Best Charity

charity   **www.BestCharity.org**
logo   **000-000-0000**

Figure 1. Sample Billboard

To find companies that rent billboard space, go to www.outdoorbillboard.com and click on the heading "Outdoor Advertising Company Directory." Then click on the state in which you want to find a billboard. From there scroll down to see the Outdoor Advertising Directory.

Broadcast Media

TV Commercial

This can be a 30-second commercial with a message from the charity founder or CEO. Show the raffle house and entice people to purchase a ticket before the deadline. The sales representative for the television network will know the best placement times for the commercial and will also provide matching PSAs at no cost.

Businesses may sponsor the commercial and have their logo and business name included; or you may allow them to use the last 10 seconds of the commercial to introduce their business. If the charity has never produced a commercial, ask your sales rep at the TV station to give you a few names of producers in the area. It usually takes about two hours to shoot and one hour to edit; they normally charge a per hour rate. Be prepared so the crew can begin filming without delay.

Another option is to speak to your area's real estate agencies that showcase their homes for sale on television. They may be willing to include the raffle house in their showcase of homes as a charitable donation or they may offer the charity a discounted rate.

Radio Commercial

Create 15-second or 30-second commercial readings. Remember this is voice and not printed so specific words are written out for the reader. You want to get a clear message out with few words. Your account representative at the station can help you with this. Write out each word because this specifically tells the reader what to say and it gives you an accurate word count. For example:

(30 second radio script – approximately 90 words)

AAA Best Charity could be your ticket to a new home! Win a 4 bedroom house or One Hundred Thousand dollars cash by supporting children in need. Tickets are a hundred dollars each, but hurry—there's only four thousand tickets total so get yours now. See the home at the open house this Sunday from 11 to 6 at 714 Silver Drive in Pleasant City, just 5 minutes from the airport. Call 000-000-0000 or go to Best Charity dot org to learn more! Paid for by _____.

(30-second radio script – approximately 90 words)

Listen everyone: Check out these odds—Win a house or One Hundred Thousand dollars cash! Only four thousand tickets will be sold – only nine hundred tickets left! You could win a beautiful 4 bedroom on a third of an acre or One Hundred Thousand dollars cash by supporting AAA Best Charity! Tickets are a hundred dollars each. Buy your ticket today at Family Bank, or online at Best Charity dot org. Paid for by _____.

(15-second radio script – approximately 40 words)

Win a 4-Bedroom house or One Hundred Thousand Dollars and support AAA Best Charity. Buy your ticket today at _____ or buy on-line at Best Charity dot org. Paid for by _____.

The PSA reel will apply here also. If you place the radio commercial on talk radio, ask if they will schedule an interview with the raffle coordinator or the home seller to talk about the house raffle on the air.

Media Interviews

Interviews should be at no charge. The marketing director, the founder of the charity, or the home seller can be interviewed. Prepare questions for the interviewer in advance so that you are sure all the points important to the house raffle get covered.

For TV or radio interviews, include information about the charity's work, a description of the house, cost of the ticket, drawing date, where to buy a ticket, and how the proceeds will benefit the charity. If you're having a ticket-sale event or an open house, also include those details in the interview. And, most importantly, don't narrow this to local stations because, remember, people across the country can purchase a ticket.

I particularly like radio for several reasons: By telephone you can be interviewed on a radio show across the United States from your bedroom—in your pajamas. Another good reason is that 96% of all Americans listen to the radio every week and 75% listen to the radio every day. This is a powerful medium for the promotion of your house raffle. Strive to get on talk radio shows for free publicity and try for the morning and evening drive-time hours for five times more response than other times of the day. Drive times are 7:30 – 8:30 AM and 5:15 – 6:15 PM.

Although you'll be working with the station's schedule for all media interviews, create a timeline as to when you would like to be interviewed and by what stations. Be flexible and willing to move at a moment's notice. You never know when a station will suddenly have an empty time slot.

Electronic Media

E-mail

Send E-mails to all previous donors. Volunteers can do this, but they should not do a mass mailing. Send the same message, but address each e-mail with the first name of the recipient in the body of the e-mail for a better response. If you produced a TV commercial, have the producer e-mail it to you so you can forward it to your list. It's a good way to tell the house raffle story.

Ask all charity employees and volunteers to send a message to everyone on their contact list. Immediate family members of charity employees cannot purchase a ticket, but friends and non-immediate family members are not excluded from purchasing a ticket. All volunteers, except Board Members, are allowed to purchase tickets. The raffle Rules and Restrictions includes an explanation of who is restricted from purchasing a ticket.

Blogs

TV stations, newspapers, and radio stations have internet blogs. They may include a snippet about your house raffle in their blogs to help the charity.

Promoting your charity makes the bloggers look like concerned citizens and benefits their image in the community too. This is just another reason to pick a charity that is well liked with a good reputation. And you can also create your own blog.

Online Advertising

I'm not an internet guru, but I know that internet marketing provides one of the best opportunities to broadcast your house raffle nationwide. Here is just a "tip of the ice-burg" list of the internet marketing you can do.

Consider placing banner ads on some or all of these sites where homebuyers go to look for homes. This is a perfect audience who may consider risking $100 to win a house.

www.Zillow.com	www.Loopnet.com
www.FSBO.com	www.Realtor.com
www.Homes.com	www.Housesforsalebycity.com

Youtube is a great place to get in front of millions of viewers. This is a site where people are entertained, informed, and inspired through the sharing of video. Youtube boasts more people visit Youtube than watch the Super Bowl, and they say that if they were Hollywood, they have enough film to release 60,000 feature films a week. I recommend that your charity consider placing a video on Youtube.

First get an account on Youtube—setting up the account is free. Type "house raffle" in Youtube's search box and view other house raffle events— this will give you a sampling of what's out there. And you can easily upload a video right from your computer. Choose "share your video with the world" or you can be selective. You can even do a self service ad with or without a video. Youtube has programs to meet almost any budget.

Banner advertising on MySpace provides exclusive targeting, so you can advertise to over 70 million U.S. users or pick a niche group based on their hobbies, interests, age, gender, and location. You can create an ad using a free template or upload your own. Send people who click on your ad to your House Raffle website and monitor the ad performance with free reports. Pricing is flexible and you control how much is spent by entering a bid for the cost per-click or cost per 1000 impressions along with a budget limit. At any time you can change the bid, the budget limit or even decide to pause a campaign.

Although many Pay Per-Click (PPC) providers exist, Google Ad Words, Yahoo! Search Marketing, and Microsoft adcenter are the three largest network operators, and all three operate under a bid-based model.

Advertise the house raffle online using these free advertising sites listed. You can even download photos of the prize home, and it's free, so use them all!

www.Craigslist.com   www.Infotube.net
www.webLeeg.com   www.Livedeal.com
www.Backpage.com   www.Postlets.com
www.Olx.com   www.Tubemogul.com
www.Usfreeads.com   www.Classifiedsforfree.com
www.50statesclassifieds.com

For all internet marketing, read their "Terms of Use" to be sure raffles or gambling are not excluded. Terms of use can change; so you want to check the latest information before you spend time with any one site.

A final secret to advertising online: If your charity is not up-to-speed with the internet, it can inexpensively hire a "computer geek" from your local high school. The charity can start by contacting the school and ask if it can make a presentation to their computer club. The charity representative can explain their interest to hire a student on the weekends—remember the students are in school so you don't want to interfere with their studies during the week. Expect that school administration will want to meet the charity representative "in person" before allowing a school visit with the students. This young computer person can be a tremendous value in helping the charity become internet savvy.

Other

Chamber of Commerce

Ask them to announce your house raffle in their newsletter and at Chamber events. Perhaps you can address business owners at a chamber meeting and discuss raffle sponsorship opportunities with them.

Santa Claus

If your raffle ticket sales happen during the holidays, then announce in the media that Santa will be taking photos with the kids at the prize home on Sunday December _____. Find a photographer and a Santa who will donate their time. Don't forget to have volunteers there as Santa's elves to sell raffle tickets. This is another way to get more people to see the prize home and support the house raffle. Charge only $5-$10 for the Santa photo to cover expenses.

Let's Dance

Throw a fundraising dance to support the raffle. You'd be surprised how many people love to dance. Contact a radio station and ask if they'll interview the house-raffle coordinator regarding the dance. Emphasize that each dance ticket includes a raffle ticket.

A church hall or community center can be used for a night of old-fashioned square dancing, country western, or fifties music. Charge more than the cost of a raffle ticket—say $115 per adult and include hors d'oeuvres and beverages.

A local band might perform at a discounted rate or use a disk jockey. Invite a restaurant to provide the hors d'oeuvres and display a banner that states that the food was sponsored by them. Make sure you get some media coverage for the event. Ticket purchasers must complete the raffle entry form to participate in the raffle. Sell the event on the charity's website with prepaid tickets, but be prepared to sell tickets at the door also. Your costs will be minimal and completely covered by that extra $30 per couple.

Charity Dinner

If the charity has a donor on its list who has a second home in a lovely vacation spot, ask if they will allow a winning couple a four-day stay. Then send invitations for dinner at a high-end restaurant to the charity's large donors. The cost should be about $1,200 per plate and it includes 10 house raffle tickets at $100 each. The door prize will be a four-day stay in the donated vacation home, and make sure the owner of the vacation home gets a free dinner. Find a local comedian who will donate the evening's entertainment. Then if one of the dinner guests happens to win the house raffle, the winner can donate the house back to the charity for a nice tax deduction, keep it, or give it to a grandchild. (Be sure to include that information on the invitation).

Celebrity Guest

Find a celebrity and invite him or her to meet and greet people in your prize home during an open house. Get media coverage, and this will increase the traffic to your open house where you can sell the raffle tickets. Movie, news, and sport celebrities in the area are excellent choices. You might ask some of the football players from your state university or a retired celebrity living in your area. Try something silly, like getting the mayor from the neighboring city to play a one-on-one basketball game against the mayor of your city at the prize home. The point is to be creative. You just want to bring a crowd. Once people see the prize home they're usually sold on buying a raffle ticket.

If you have celebrities who live in your area, go online and locate their agents who will connect you with their publicists. Send the publicist an e-mail about your charity and the house raffle. This search takes a little noodling around on the internet; but if you're successful in bringing a celebrity, it can significantly pump up the ticket sales. Think of the celebrities who have said publicly that they believe in your charity's cause. For example, Betty White is an avid animal welfare activist.

It's unrealistic to expect a major celebrity to fly across the United States to meet and greet people at your open house; but if film and television production takes place in your state, then find out which actors are working locally. Then focus on getting in touch with the actor's publicist and find out if the celebrity would have time to attend an Open House. Although weekends are best, be willing to hold your Open House at a time and day that fits best with the celebrity's schedule.

Open Houses

To comply with Raffle Rules and Restrictions, you must hold at least one Open House so that the grand prize is available for viewing by the public. Use the Open House as a wonderful opportunity for potential ticket buyers not only to view the prize home, but to get excited about the possibility of winning it for only $100 and buy more tickets. STEP 12 includes specific ways to enhance the Open House event to increase ticket sales.

Follow-up Meeting
with the Charity

T he follow-up meeting is the time to finalize areas to be sure everyone is in agreement moving forward. In addition, a few new items need to be addressed. If you find that you'll require more meeting times with the charity, then schedule them as needed.

At this meeting you need to review the following:

1. The charity's marketing plan
2. Expenses
3. Home seller's involvement
4. Ticket sales formula
5. Ticket sales minimum requirement
6. Extension of the drawing date if this becomes necessary
7. Escrow Holding Account
8. Ticket Sales Start Date
9. Raffle Rules and Restrictions

Charity's Marketing Plan

Review the marketing plan created by the charity to be sure it is a comprehensive plan. Discuss their advertising budget to fulfill this plan, either on their own or through sponsors. If sponsors will be used, then they must be in place prior to the start of the raffle. If the marketing plan is weak, you might refer to the promotional ideas outlined in the previous chapter and suggest incorporating some of those items. With a tight budget, choose ideas that require little cash output.

Expenses

Are there available funds to cover all of the raffle expenses? The following are some of the basic expenses that the charity will need to consider:

- Marketing costs to cover all items included in the raffle marketing plan

- Printing costs of tickets, rules, entry forms, thank-you letters and fliers

- The cost to create a website

- Postage for any planned mailings

- Credit card fee charges on ticket purchases

- Any additional staff time

Home Seller's Involvement

Discuss your role in the sale of raffle tickets and promoting the raffle. In a house raffle, the involvement of the home seller is a matter of *need and agreement*. In other words, maybe the charity has an in-house task force and an advertising budget to handle it all, and there is no need for the home seller to be actively involved in ticket sales or promoting the raffle. The home seller can provide the grand prize and nothing more. Conversely, if it fits, the home seller can receive compensation and take over specific functions of the raffle process. So partner with the members of your charity and make an arrangement with them that will accomplish the goal of completing a successful raffle for both of you. At the same time, be careful that you're not taking on the full burden because if you overwhelm yourself, you will have a problem succeeding.

If your schedule does not permit you to be actively involved, then you must be sure that the charity can handle it all. Don't become confused and think that the money the charity is going to pay you from the raffle proceeds includes your becoming the raffle coordinator—it doesn't. You're giving the charity your house in exchange for that money. So be sure you give your involvement careful consideration, and create a win/win situation.

In the next step when the charity and the homeowner complete the necessary paperwork, the extent of the homeowner's involvement will be clearly defined in writing.

Finalize the Ticket Sale Formula

Refer to the ticket sales formula that you created earlier which included the home sale price, total number of tickets, ticket sale price, other prizes, and the profit amount to the charity. This is the same formula that you presented to the charity at the first meeting. Be sure that you have a ticket sale price that matches the prize, the least amount of total tickets necessary to cover all costs, the price of the home plus encumbrances, and a nice cash reward for the charity. Be sure that your sale price falls within the current fair market value of comparable sold properties in your area. Now is the time to make any adjustments to the formula.

Discuss the possibility of fewer tickets being sold. The goal is to get all available tickets sold; however, if fewer are sold, could the charity proceed with the drawing and be satisfied with the profit from this fundraiser? Find out from your charity how many tickets they need to sell in order to cover expenses as well as the purchase price of the home and still make a satisfactory profit for their organization. I call this number the *ticket sales minimum requirement.*

Drawing Date Extension

In the event that the ticket sales minimum requirement is not met prior to the drawing date, then an extension of the drawing date may be needed. While it's impossible to determine an exact extension date at this time, the possibility of an extension should be discussed so that you can be prepared. The Raffle Rules and Restrictions specify only one 60-day extension is allowed.

A later step provides detailed information about the extension of a raffle drawing and creating raffle tickets; right now discussion should include the possibility of an extension and how it would impact the bottom-line expenses. The state in which my house was raffled required that the drawing date be printed on the ticket but the drawing date can easily be changed on the ticket confirmation before it is sent to future ticket buyers. Your official tickets are on cardstock, cut to size, possibly color, etc and much more expensive to reprint, so print the official tickets later when you are sure of the final drawing date.

In the Raffle Rules and Restrictions, there are several places to insert the drawing date; and later on in this meeting, you will fill in the blanks. This date can also be changed easily on the Raffle Rules and Restrictions in the event of an extension and given out to new ticket buyers.

Escrow Holding Account

For the protection of both parties, an escrow account must be set up to hold the raffle funds coming in. Unlike other fund raisers run by the charity, this one is unique. All the money coming in doesn't belong to the charity—in essence; the charity is holding your money; that is the price it is going to pay you for your home at the successful completion of the raffle. Any payment to compensate the homeowner for working on the raffle will also be paid through the escrow account. Setting up an escrow account to hold the raffle funds is *a nonnegotiable element.*

The escrow holding account should require a minimum of three signatures for any money to be removed, with one of the signatures being you, the Seller. The Seller should have the right to view statements on the account at any time. Be sure to include instructions that the escrow company will send certified funds required for closing the sale of the home directly to your settlement company.

At no time is the money raised from ticket sales to be in your name, and at no time does the charity have control over the money either. This arrangement safeguards both parties. Any interest earned on the funds will belong to the charity.

Ticket Sales Start Date

Make a final decision on the start date to begin selling tickets and the date you want to wrap-up ticket sales. Consider the information provided earlier regarding the best and worst times to be selling raffle tickets. Be sure that you and the charity have time to make all necessary preparations before the start date. Remember that the prize home must be ready, also, and keep in mind the extension period if it becomes necessary.

Raffle Rules and Restrictions

Go through each line of the Raffle Rules and Restrictions, and fill in the blanks for your house raffle. This will require decisions in several areas, such as the drawing date, prizes beyond the Grand prize, specifics for claiming the prize, and the method chosen for confirming that all ticket numbers are in the container (see STEP 13 under "Address Their Concerns" for ticket-confirming methods). Also, double-check to be sure any specific needs of your raffle are addressed. Incorporate any requirements of your state. Registering the raffle with the State Attorney General's office is usually required, and the charity can get the specific instructions for this by calling the Attorney General's office or by checking the Attorney General's website for the appropriate form.

▶ Congratulations!
You're ready to seal the deal.

Sealing the Deal

S ome states use a title company that provides escrow services to handle the closing of a real estate sale. In other states a real estate attorney, an escrow company, or a loan officer handles this function. For simplicity, I've used the name title company in my instructions. Use the type of settlement agent for your area.

The home seller and the charity will need to sign two documents. One is the Real Estate Purchase Agreement for the house and the second is the Win-a-House Raffle Agreement. Before signing, ask the charity to provide you with a copy of their *Resolution of Authority.* This document outlines who has the legal authority to sign for the charity. Only authorized parties should sign the agreements.

Sign a Purchase Agreement

This is an agreement between you (the Seller) and the charity (the Buyer) of your home. If you are represented by a real estate agent in this sale, then your agent will provide you with the standard purchase agreement used in your state and walk you through the process of completing it. If you're working without an agent, you can get a real estate purchase agreement at a local office supply store, a form store, or buy one online. This is the same form you would use if you were selling your home to a qualified buyer in the conventional way. (A sample Purchase Agreement can be found in Appendices C and D).

If you have never sold a home, or you just don't feel comfortable filling out this form, then pay a real estate agent to do this with you. A bank or title company can also help you fill out a purchase agreement.

The purchase agreement contains several elements: purchase price, earnest money, settlement signing date, closing costs, home warranty, inspections, and addendums. Take a look at the following elements of a purchase agreement.

Purchase price

This is the price you calculated based on the market evaluation of your property. This price, which included your holding costs and encumbrances, is the same price you outlined in your meetings with the charity.

Earnest Money

This money from the charity can be waived. However, you can ask for a non-refundable deposit so the charity knows it will lose this money if it doesn't successfully meet the ticket sales minimum requirement and complete the raffle. If you ask for earnest money, I recommend $1,000 to $2,000. The check for the earnest money should be certified funds made out to the title company. For my raffle, I waived any earnest money from the charity. Do what feels right for your situation.

Settlement Signing Date

This is the date when you and the charity will close on the escrow of the sale. The settlement signing date should be "on or before 35 days" from the raffle drawing. This gives enough time for a qualified winner to claim the prize and for you and the charity to close on the sale of the home with the title company.

Closing Costs

The closing costs for the charity should be paid by you—the seller. Normally, the buyer and seller share in the closing costs; but remember, the raffle is meant to benefit the charity, so you will need to be generous. Since this is an all-cash buy, fees associated with a lender are eliminated. You may want to call the title company in advance to find out a very close estimate as to the actual closing costs involved. Again, remember if you had sold your home through conventional means, you may not get your asking price for the home and you would still pay your share of the closing costs. So don't be concerned about paying the charity's closing costs. This is not money that you will bring to closing; it is money that will be deducted from your payout amount from the sale price of your home.

Home Warranty

Obtaining a home warranty is important because the charity will want to feel comfortable that the winner is going to be happy with their prize and won't be hit with a bunch of home repairs. Include in the purchase agreement that you, the Seller, will provide a home warranty. Unless you were brave and your raffle home is a fixer-upper in a sought-after area, then you would include in the purchase agreement that the home is offered "as is without warranty."

Inspections

The charity may want some preliminary inspections done and the Home Warranty company, chosen by the home seller, will also inspect prior to providing the warranty. If the home seller agrees to cure any objections from the charity buyer, any such objections must be cured approximately 10 days after the resolution deadline. In an ordinary home sale, the seller cures objections prior to the settlement closing date, but in a house raffle, the charity buyer cannot wait until just prior to the closing of the sale which would be after the drawing. The charity needs to know before accepting a house as its grand prize that any serious objections to the sale have been cured.

Raffle Contingency Addendum

Attach an addendum to the purchase agreement that reads:

Addendum No. (1)
This purchase agreement is contingent on the successful completion of the Buyer's house raffle on (insert drawing date). In the event that

Buyer does not sell (insert ticket sales minimum requirement amount,) this purchase agreement will be voided and Buyer will not suffer any penalties except for the loss of the earnest money.

If you did not ask for earnest money from the charity, there is no loss and the addendum is still accurate as written.

Escrow Holding Account Addendum

Attach an addendum to the purchase agreement that reads:

Addendum No. (2)
This purchase agreement dated, (insert date of signing) is contingent on the Buyer and Seller setting up an escrow account to hold all funds from ticket sales until the successful completion of the raffle or at such time as the raffle is canceled. The escrow account will be set up at (insert name of escrow company) within _____ days of the date of this purchase agreement.

Lead-Based Paint Addendum

Lead was used in house paint prior to 1978. You should complete a lead-based paint disclosure form whether the home was built before 1978 or not. This is simple to do, and it protects you. (A sample Lead-Based Paint Disclosure form can be found in Appendix F). You can also download a Lead-Based Paint Disclosure form at www.hud.gov/offices/lead/library/enforcement/selr_eng.pdf

Extending the Drawing Date

In the event that the raffle drawing is extended, the purchase agreement will require a new addendum that states that the drawing date and the real estate closing date have been extended. Include the new dates in the addendum which must be signed by the charity (Buyer) and the homeowner (Seller).

The new dates will have to be agreed upon by both parties. You don't want to sign or attach any such addendum now because you don't know for certain that you will need to extend or just how long the extension should be.

▶ Prepare for rain, but expect your picnic
to take place in the glorious sunshine as planned.
The plan is to get all the tickets sold
by the original drawing date,
get your house sold at your asking price,
and provide a nice cash reward
to a charity you believe in.

After the purchase agreement is signed, make a copy for the charity and provide the charity with a disclosure statement for your property. Property disclosure statement forms can be purchased online, or at a form or office supply store. This is a form in which the seller discloses what they know about the condition of the property. Each state can have its own unique property disclosure form. This is because each area has specific challenges from climate, geography, and building codes. Appendix E includes a sample page from a property disclosure statement.

Your house is now officially off the market; you have a pending sale. The price you put on the purchase agreement, like that of any pending sale, needs to remain confidential. Why? Because if the pending sale falls out, then you might end up putting your house on the market at a later date; and you don't want the price you agreed to with the charity to be a price you are tied to in the future.

You are handling the sale of your home just like any other sale of real estate except that you are pushing back the sale closing date until the charity raises the funds through ticket sales to pay for the house. Move forward with the action items of the real estate purchase agreement to include ordering any property inspections and a title commitment. The home seller will order the title commitment and the charity will have a set number of days to object to title exceptions. The charity must be sure that any objectionable exceptions to the title can be satisfied prior to accepting the home as the grand prize for the raffle.

Sign a Win-a-House Raffle Agreement

This is an agreement between the homeowner and the charity that outlines their arrangement as it pertains to the raffle. The agreement explains what happens at the conclusion of the raffle; and it includes any specific functions the homeowner has agreed to handle in regards to ticket sales or the promotion of the raffle. The agreement also outlines any compensation to the homeowner for this work; and if the homeowner will not take an active roll in ticket sales or the promotion of the raffle, this is also stated in the Win-a-House Raffle Agreement. (A sample Win-a-House Raffle Agreement can be found in Appendix G).

The homeowner involvement I'm referring to does not relate to the homeowner informing friends and co-workers about the house raffle but it relates to a more involved capacity, for instance, holding open houses, distributing fliers, producing a commercial, calling on sponsors or paying for any advertising.

Should the raffle be canceled, the charity will *not* be liable to pay the homeowner for their work on the raffle unless otherwise agreed. This is the time for the charity and the homeowner to come to a clear understanding and solidify the arrangement and put it in writing. Any payment to the homeowner for their work on the raffle must be paid by certified funds through the escrow holding account prior to any winners receiving any prize. This protects both parties. It ensures that the charity has the funds available to pay the homeowner, and it ensures that the homeowner does not have to try and collect this amount at a later time.

Sign the Win-a-House Raffle Agreement with the charity at the same time that you sign the purchase agreement for the home. The steps that follow, and the sample Win-a-House Raffle Agreement in the appendices, coincide with the charity closing the sale with the home seller and accepting title to the property even if the grand prize winner chooses the cash option instead of the home. However, if the home seller and the charity agreed to a holding fee payable to the home seller instead of the charity taking title, then both parties should execute a separate holding fee agreement before the start of ticket sales.

I recommend that a qualified attorney prepare the necessary documents so the purchase agreement for the home is properly tied to the holding fee agreement. Be sure your state has no restrictions in this regard.

Register the Raffle

After any objections to the purchase of the home have been satisfied, then the charity can register the raffle and begin selling tickets. Most states require that the raffle be registered with the State Attorney General's office. Remember, nonprofit organizations can hold raffles, individuals cannot. Therefore, the charity is the one that will register the raffle. The charity can contact the office of the State Attorney General and obtain the instructions for registering the raffle, or it can locate the appropriate form on the Attorney General's website.

You may find that your State Attorney General's office does not require that you register the raffle, but the gaming control board of your state may require that you submit an application or obtain a license. The state in which my house was raffled did not require that the nonprofit obtain a license unless it was going to hold a raffle more than four times in one year. Otherwise, the nonprofit is required to submit a raffle request and report form if the prize was over $75,000. So the nonprofit organization should closely follow the state requirements in this regard.

The Ticket Sale System

I t will help the marketing process if the charity promotes its cause by creating a name for the raffle such as Save the Planet—Win a House Raffle. This name can be on the house raffle website as well as on all marketing materials and the entry form. Then follow a simple system for selling and tracking ticket sales.

The Process

After ticket buyers have the opportunity to read the Raffle Rules and Restrictions for the raffle, they purchase a ticket by completing an entry form and providing payment. Once payment is verified, the ticket, a copy of the Raffle Rules and Restrictions, and a thank-you-for-participating letter are provided to the ticket purchaser. This is a simple process except for one thing, the United States Postal Service prohibits the mailing of raffle or lottery tickets—this is a federal law mandated by congress. You will find that many house raffles continue to mail the raffle ticket so it appears that the law is not strictly enforced, but some house raffles mail an unofficial copy of the ticket or a ticket receipt or voucher while others are e-mailing a copy of the ticket.

I recommend that you keep the official ticket to place into the raffle container at the time of the drawing and mail or e-mail a "ticket confirmation" which is a larger version of the actual official ticket. Later on I'll explain the specifics of what to put on the ticket, and the look of the ticket and the ticket confirmation.

Entry Form Particulars

If you have credit card machines for your "in person ticket sale locations," such as the Open House, then use an entry form at those sites that doesn't require the ticket buyer to write in their credit card number, the CVV code and signature. Swiping the card eliminates the need to have that information on the entry form, and it provides additional security for the ticket buyer. The sample entry forms in Appendices H and I show both types of forms.

Now become familiar with the following particulars regarding ticket buyers and the completion of the entry form:

- People may purchase more than one ticket.

- Individuals may join together and purchase one or more tickets.

- In the event that more than one name or group of individuals is listed on the winning ticket entry form, the first name listed will be deemed the winner. It is the sole responsibility of the winner to allocate any such prize shares to other participants in the multiple parties listed.

- Board members or employees of the charity, employees and agents of the homeowner, and immediate family members of any of the preceding are not eligible to participate in the drawing. Any tickets purchased by such will be void.

- Entrants must be 18 years or older and have a valid Social Security number which will be verified before awarding any prize.

- Ticket buyers should print neatly, provide complete information, and verify the accuracy of the information entered on the entry form as this information will be used to locate them if they win a prize.

- Ticket buyers may pay for a ticket and put a different name on the entry form.

Sometimes ticket buyers pay the cost of the ticket, but want the prize awarded to someone other than themselves. This may happen in the case of parents buying for an adult child, which is not a problem. The winner is the name on the entry form and that person must meet the requirements to qualify. Be careful here, though; you cannot have a winner who is under 18 years of age according to the Raffle Rules and Restrictions. However, if the ticket buyer wants to award the prize to a minor, then the ticket buyer may give the prize to whomever they choose after taking possession of the prize.

There is no need for ticket sellers to check documentation to be sure ticket buyers meet the qualifications to purchase a ticket. Before any prize is awarded, the charity will verify qualifications. However, in the event that a youthful looking individual attempts to purchase a ticket in person, the individual should be informed of the age requirement.

The last item on the Raffle Rules and Restrictions is, "Void where prohibited." To avoid any problems, I would return or not accept ticket purchases coming from states where raffles are illegal. There are only a few states that do not allow raffles, and you can easily list those states on your website. It's a bit confusing because residents of Hawaii, where gambling is illegal, may go to a casino in Las Vegas and gamble; so if they come to your open house and buy a ticket, they're not in Hawaii, so shouldn't that be okay? It would be difficult to keep track of whether a person purchased across state lines or while they were in your state. And the game isn't over yet; you must send them the ticket confirmation after their payment is processed, and then the drawing needs to take place at a later date.

The attorney I conferred with on this issue, advised to keep it safe and simple void where prohibited. One place to check for states that do not allow raffles is at www.rafflefaq.com/united-states-raffle-laws

Thank-You-For-Participating Letter

In the thank-you letter, the charity should take advantage of this great opportunity to help the ticket buyer learn more about the charity's good work. Some ticket buyers may have heard about the charity only by virtue of the house raffle; so this is a chance to send information to recipients who will definitely open the envelope or the e-mail as they anticipate the arrival of their ticket confirmation. However, this isn't a time for the charity to ask for a donation, but a time to build on this relationship for the future.

See the following example of a thank-you-for-participating letter.

Dear Supporter,

Thank you for participating in our Win-a-House fundraiser. Your official ticket is retained to be placed in the raffle container at the time of the drawing. Enclosed are your ticket confirmation and a copy of the Raffle Rules and Restrictions.

By purchasing this ticket you are helping homeless and abandoned children of Southern California find homes where they will be cherished. AAA Best Charity provides foster homes, medical and dental care, and placement services for over 1,200 children each year. With the proceeds from the house raffle, we anticipate adding more foster care homes and psychological trauma therapy for our children.

Open Houses at the prize home will be held the first Sunday of each month from 11:00 a.m. to 6:00 p.m. Please continue to let others know about the house raffle. Full information and places to buy tickets are listed on our website at www.00000.org.

The Drawing is scheduled for November 17, 2010. The winner does not have to be present to win, however, you are invited to attend, and we welcome your family and friends to join the celebration.

Good luck and thank you for your support.

Cordially,

Figure 2. Sample Thank-You-For-Participating Letter

If the charity wants to save postage costs for mailings, then they may choose to only e-mail copies of the ticket confirmation, however, some people still do not have access to the internet so keep that in mind.

The Look of the Ticket

Include the following information on the Official Ticket:

- Ticket number in bold type (tickets must be consecutively numbered).

- The word "raffle" (Do not write words such as gift or donation).

- Name of the nonprofit organization

- List of prizes. If you have many prizes beyond the prize home, just state it in general terms, for example, over $25,000 in other prizes.

- Address of the prize home and a brief description such as 4 Bedroom Home valued at $_____.

- Date, Time, Place of drawing.

- The cost of the ticket.

- Any additional information required by your state.

If your state does not require that you type the place of the drawing on the ticket, I recommend that you don't include the location so that you will have more time to determine an appropriate location after you have a better feeling of the number of people who may attend the drawing. The charity can advertise the drawing location on its website a few weeks before the drawing date.

The Official ticket will be kept and placed in the raffle container for the drawing. In order for all the tickets to fit in the drum, make this ticket small. Print it on card stock with the ticket number at 14 point font size, and the rest of the information at 8 point font size. Wait to print the official tickets until you're positive you won't need an extension so that the official ticket has the final drawing date on it. The following is an example of an Official Ticket:

Ticket No. 1875   OFFICIAL

AAA Best Charity House Raffle
Ticket Cost: $100, Prizes: 4 Bedroom Home valued at
$250,000 located at 777 Silver Dr. Forest, New Mexico
or $100,000 cash plus $25,000 in other prizes.
Drawing Date/Time: May 12, 2010 at 3:00 pm MST.
Drawing Location: 777 Silver Dr., Forest, New Mexico

Figure 3. Sample Official Ticket

The ticket confirmation that you send to the ticket buyer, after their payment has been verified, will have the same information on it but enlarged. It will not be printed on cardstock. You can also add more information to the ticket confirmation such as a list of sponsors, contact information, and added instructions. The following is an example of a ticket confirmation, or "unofficial ticket."

Ticket No. 1875   **Ticket Confirmation**

AAA Best Charity House Raffle
Ticket Cost: $100
Prizes: 4 Bedroom Home valued at $250,000 located at: 777 Silver Dr.
Forest, New Mexico or $100,000 cash PLUS $25,000 in other prizes.
Drawing Date/Time: May 12, 2010 at 3:00 pm MST
Drawing Location: 777 Silver Dr., Forest, New Mexico

Thank you to our sponsors: XXX Best Plumbing, XXX Best Printer,
XXX Best Home Mortgage, XXX Pet Store, XXX Best Furniture
-Prize winners do not have to be present to win.
-The actual "official ticket" will be placed in the raffle container for the drawing.
-You are not required to present this copy—your name is logged with this ticket No.
-For additional raffle information call: 000-000-0000

Figure 4. Sample Ticket Confirmation

Your printer will be your best guide on how to print a cheap ticket; or maybe you can ask a printer to donate the printing and include the printer's name as a sponsor on the ticket confirmation. Explain that approximately 4,000 people (or your ticket amount) will see the printer's name. Your local printer can print raffle tickets that are consecutively numbered for the official ticket.

There are many companies that also sell printed raffle tickets. I don't recommend those tickets unless you customize the ticket to fit your needs. Many raffle equipment company tickets have a tear-off stub where the ticket buyer keeps one part of the ticket and the raffle holder keeps the other part. The portion that the raffle holder keeps is small and doesn't provide space for all the information that is needed. For this reason, you are using an entry form; in essence, this is your portion of the ticket that will be matched to the official ticket at the drawing.

If there is an extension of the drawing date, ticket buyers who purchased before the extension will have the original drawing date on their copy of the Raffle Rules and Restrictions; nevertheless, the Raffle Rules and Restrictions state that there can be an extension, and these ticket buyers will have received a written notification of the new date so this should not cause a problem. Some states require that you provide a sample of your ticket for approval. To avoid any glitches, I recommend that you submit a ticket sample of both the ticket confirmation, and the official ticket.

Raffle Website

As I mentioned before, it's best to create a website solely dedicated to the house raffle and not part of the charity's existing site. Make the website simple, don't crowd it, and make it an easy process for ticket buyers to get the information they need and purchase a ticket. The house raffle website should include:

- The raffle name

- A line that says the charity is a nonprofit tax exempt organization

- A statement that the net profit from the raffle proceeds will go to the charity

- A line or two of how the funds will help the charity's cause

- A picture and description of the prize home (include the address)

- A virtual tour of the home if possible

- A list of ways the buyer can get a ticket

- The entry form "without a credit card machine" that viewers can download and mail in

- The ability to purchase online by credit card

- A running total of how many tickets have been sold and how many total tickets can be sold

- The raffle Rules and Restrictions that viewers can download

A company that creates virtual tours may be willing to create a home tour at no cost because its company name will be advertised on the virtual tour. Remember, your raffle will get exposure; so this is added advertising for any business that supports the raffle. At the raffle of my house, a gracious ticket buyer at our first Open House volunteered to donate a virtual tour of the prize home. We accepted.

Note: As the home seller, you want to be sure the charity is able to follow through by getting all the tickets sold. If the charity fails, you won't get your house sold, and you will have wasted precious time having your house off the market for months. You don't want this to happen. As previously mentioned, you might be in a position to help the charity because everybody wins if this is handled properly and the raffle is a success.

Places to Buy Tickets

For the best possible ticket sales, make sure people can buy tickets in several places. These include in-person places to go, online purchasing, fax, and mail. When I raffled my house, we sold tickets at four walk-in places: two banks, the charity's office, and at the charity's adoption desk inside a large pet store. Charity employees handled the tickets at the pet store and at the charity's office, and bank employees handled the ticket sales within the bank. One bank even had a table displaying the work of the charity and a miniature house.

The bank where the charity has an account might be willing to sell tickets in the bank, deposit the money directly into the charity's account, and then wire the money to the escrow holding company. A poster or display could be set up in the bank lobby. If the bank knows its name will be used on promotional materials and in radio and TV advertisements directing people to come to the bank to buy tickets, it will see this as value added and will most likely agree to sell tickets in the bank. If the charity's bank is unwilling to sell tickets in the bank, the charity might consider opening another account at a bank that will.

Ticket buyers who don't want to use a credit card online can download the entry form and fax or mail it to the charity.

▶ The world is full of busy people.
Make it easy for them to buy,
and your ticket sales will move quickly.

Fliers with Entry Form

The fliers being distributed should be two-sided with the entry form printed on the backside for mailing or faxing. Use the entry form "without a credit card machine." Be sure that the entry form on the back of the flier shows the return deadline, which should be *10 days prior to the drawing*. You want to wrap up ticket sales 10 days before the drawing because you don't want mailed-in checks arriving when the tickets are all sold out. Returning late-arriving payments only adds to the cost of the raffle. If you're not completely sold out 10 days prior, you can continue to sell online, by phone, or in person using instant payments such as cash or credit cards. Ten days prior to the drawing, you don't have time to wait for checks to clear.

Keeping Track

Use a Ticket Sales Log Sheet to track ticket sales. The charity can create a computerized spreadsheet similar to my sample log sheet for easy tracking. (A sample ticket sales log sheet can be found in Appendix J). Number it in advance beginning with 1 to the total number of tickets to be sold. As a ticket is sold, insert the name of the ticket buyer, date, and form of payment next to the ticket number.

It is helpful if the charity keeps a chart that graphs the marketing methods being used coinciding with the number of tickets coming in daily. This helps demonstrate which promotional methods are working best. Repeat the methods that are pulling in the most number of ticket sales.

Raffle Hot-Line

Set up a raffle hotline with a recorded phone message with a list of the most commonly asked questions and the answers to them. This phone number can be printed on fliers and any print advertising. This will prevent the charity from being inundated with phone calls. There are still many people who do not have internet access, and this is a way for them to get their questions answered. Also, others don't want to read through the entire Raffle Rules and Restrictions to get informed. Here are a few sample questions:

- Where is the prize home?

- What is the home like?

- Do I need to be present to win?

- Can I purchase more than one ticket?

- Can I live out of state and still buy a ticket?

- When is the drawing date?

- What forms of payment are accepted?

- When can I see the prize home?

- Do I have to pay taxes on the winnings?

- Where can I buy tickets?

Make sure you still provide a way for people to speak with the raffle coordinator just in case their questions aren't covered or they have other concerns. Be careful, also, that only persons informed about the raffle details address people's questions; otherwise, you can have a problem brewing if people get conflicting answers. You want only positive publicity for your house raffle.

▶ The snowman's belly has been formed,
now roll it around in the snow,
and let it get big and fat!

Oops! He's Not Fat Enough!

S ometimes, even though ticket sales have been moving, the ticket sales minimum requirement is not going to be reached by the drawing date. In such cases, at least two weeks before the scheduled drawing date, you need to make the decision to extend.

Extending the Drawing Date

Calculate how many tickets are selling per day and how many additional days you will need to reach the goal. Also, consider the time of year the drawing is being held. For instance, if the drawing was scheduled for November 15, ticket sales will slow down after the holidays. Raffles should be extended only once; otherwise, the public will become disheartened and request a refund. Extensions should be reasonable too, approximately 30 to 45 days and not more than 60 days.

The sample Raffle Rules and Restrictions in Appendix B indicates that the Raffle drawing date can be extended for up to 60 days. If you're not sure how many days you'll need, extend for the full 60 days to allow for ample time to get the remaining tickets sold. Be sure that you have checked on any restrictions pertaining to raffle extensions applicable to your state.

The charity should send a simple letter informing ticket purchasers of the extension. Don't be too apologetic in the letter; you don't want ticket purchasers to think there is a problem and request a refund. There is no problem; the charity just needs a little more time to get the remaining tickets sold. This letter can be sent by U.S. mail or by electronic mail and should be typed on the charity's letterhead. The extension letter should come from the charity's executive director or founder—not from the homeowner. See the following example of a letter to extend the drawing date.

August 15, 2010

Dear Ticket Buyer:

We're close to reaching our goal of ticket sales for the WIN-A-HOUSE RAFFLE benefiting AAA Best Charity but we're not quite there. To ensure that we have a winner, the drawing date has been extended to:

Date: October 4, 2010
Time: 1:00 pm, Mountain Standard Time
Place: At the prize home located at 714 Silver Dr., Pleasant City, New Mexico

The winner does not need to be present to win, but we invite everyone to join us in the celebration. Please continue to support our ticket sales efforts in one or more of the following ways:

- Tell your neighbors, friends, and co-workers about the house raffle.
- Bring a neighbor, friend, or co-worker to an open house.
- Send an e-mail to everyone on your e-mail list.
- Increase your odds by purchasing another ticket.

Out-of-state friends and family can participate as well, so don't forget to tell everyone about the house raffle. You will find the number of actual remaining tickets posted on our website at www.00000.org

Thank you for your participation, and we look forward to awarding this wonderful prize to the lucky winner on October 4th.

Cordially,
Carolyn Helper
Executive Director

Figure 5. Sample Extension Letter

Extend the drawing date in your purchase agreement by attaching an addendum stating that Buyer and Seller agree to the extension of the raffle drawing. Review the purchase agreement and include all applicable dates in your addendum. Both Buyer (the charity) and Seller (homeowner) must sign the addendum. Change the drawing date for all ticket confirmations being sent to ticket buyers. If you followed my advice, and haven't printed the Official Tickets yet, then you can continue to hold until you are sure the minimum number of tickets required for a successful drawing will be achieved by the new date. Then print the Official Tickets with the final drawing date on them.

▶ Keep selling those tickets!
Review your marketing plan and repeat what's
making the greatest impact on ticket sales.

Pushing Ticket Sales –
The Open House

I found that the Open House brought in more ticket sales than any other form of paid advertising. They take some effort and preparation, but with little cost you can get an added "push" in ticket sales. The following Open House system was perfected over time; I highly recommend that you copy it.

Schedule the Open House on a Sunday from 11:00 am – 6:00 p.m. on a good weather day. Fewer people will come in the rain or snow. Also, some people work on Sundays and they will appreciate the extra hour to be able to make it to your Open House.

Stage the home. If this is an empty house, see if a local furniture store would be willing to take advantage of a golden opportunity to stage the home. Remember, this allows them to place brochures advertising their store throughout the home so they should do it at no cost. You can mention the furniture store's name in any of your Open House advertising. The entire house does not have to be staged; concentrate on the main living areas such as the living room and dining room. Place other simple items in bathrooms and in the kitchen such as flowers, towels, a bowl of fruit, cookbooks etc. If this is not an empty house, then be sure it is clean, and not cluttered. Put away any valuables.

Let the Public Know About Your Open House

In the week leading up to the Open House, prepare and distribute fliers, send out press releases, run ads in the newspaper, create signs, and post a message on the raffle website.

Open House Flier

Create a flier announcing the Open House. You can find a sample flier in Appendix L. For one week prior to the Open House have local businesses stuff your flier into customer bags. One week in advance is sufficient, because if you distribute fliers earlier than one week, people will have forgotten about the event and the flier will have been misplaced.

Volunteers can place fliers on car windshields (if this doesn't violate any local ordinance) in parking lots of businesses throughout the city. Also, distribute these fliers while the Open House is in progress so that people who are already out can just make a quick pass over to the Open House as it happens. Remember those busy people; catch them when they are just minutes from your event.

Press Releases

Send a press release to local newspapers, TV, or radio stations. The press release should include information about the charity, how the funds will help its cause, a description of the prize home, and the Open House time and place. Charities survive on fundraising; so the marketing director will have the resources to issue a press release.

Newspaper Advertisement

The newspaper may have an online calendar of events where you can include the information about the Open House at no cost. Also, run an ad in the newspaper to appear on the day of the Open House. If the newspapers are already doing a story that includes the Open House information, then just place a line ad in the classified Real Estate section for Open Houses, (Figures 3 and 4 show examples). Be sure to include your raffle hotline phone number in the ad.

AS SEEN ON KKK TV
ONLY $100, Win a 4 Bd. on 1/3 acre
Or choose $100,000.00 CASH
Only 845 tickets left.
Only 4,000 tickets will be sold!
OPEN 11 a.m. - 6 p.m.
714 Silver Dr. (I-57 north, west on Silver)
Benefiting AAA Best Charity
(000) 000-0000

Figure 6. Sample Newspaper Ad

DROP DEAD GORGEOUS!
ONLY $100, Win a 4 Bd. on 1/3 acre,
Or choose $100,000.00 CASH
Only 845 ticket left.
Only 4,000 tickets will be sold!
OPEN 11 a.m. - 6 p.m.
714 Silver Dr. (I-57north, west on Silver)
Benefiting AAA Best Charity
(000) 000-0000

Figure 7. Sample Newspaper Ad

Avoid the temptation to save money by overly abbreviating your ads. The newspaper representative may suggest their standard abbreviations; and real estate agents' ads are packed with them, but too many abbreviations can make it difficult for people to read and understand. Also, even if the same area code is used throughout your state, include it in the phone number because out-of-state people can pull up the ad online.

Open House Signs

On the morning of the Open House, line your main cross-streets with at least 40 signs leading people to the prize home. Yes, I really meant forty signs—the Open House sign is your most valuable tool. The reason for 40 signs is that this is a unique event; it's not an ordinary open house where someone is selling a house. As people see sign after sign, they'll know that something special is going on, and they should probably check it out. Remember the signs are covering the area in all directions to the prize home, so one person may see only 8 to 10 signs—not all 40.

Making the Open House Sign

The signs are easy to make and offer some of the best advertising for the Open House. Follow these instructions to make your signs.

From a sign store purchase blank, white corrugated signs (24" wide x 18" tall) with metal stakes and small red Open House directional arrow signs with metal stakes. These red directional signs are usually 6" x 24" and are also carried at large home improvement stores. Don't forget to ask if the sign store owner will support the raffle by providing a nonprofit discount price to the charity. Then buy a red and a blue permanent marker and a permanent wide black marker. (Office supply stores carry a wide black marker called Sharpie MAGNUM). Buy red balloons, one for each sign plus a few extras, a helium tank, and a string of pendent flags which will be used later.

Using the address of your prize home, write the following message on both sides of your sign in black ink, in three lines.

4 Bd. House

Only $100

714 Silver Dr.

The important point here is to put as little information on the sign as possible, but enough to give people a reason to come so you can explain to them what you're doing. The whole story cannot be told on a sign that people are trying to read from a moving vehicle. I'm sure you've been frustrated by signs with print that no one could possibly read from a distance. Remember that full information is on your fliers, in live interviews, and newspaper ads.

Use your blue and red markers to underline the words "only $100" several times. Then insert the separate Open House directional arrow sign at the top. Looking at a street map, decide where the signs should be placed—include one in front of the prize home. Then cut off the point of the arrow on the red directional open house sign for all signs that won't be placed at intersections requiring a turn or that won't be on the same street where the house is located. Only signs that will be placed at intersections requiring a turn and signs on the same street as the prize home should have the arrow point.

Place the signs that don't have the arrow point facing oncoming traffic. This allows the driver to see the sign from a distance, without having to look sideways. Save the signs with the point of the arrow still intact for the intersections where you want people to make a turn and for the street where the prize home is located. (Check with City Code Enforcement for any restrictions on sign placement).

Tie a red inflated balloon to the top of each sign. Don't make the string too long, 12 inches above the sign is good. The movement of the balloon will catch the public's eye; but if it's placed too high above the sign, people won't have time to look down and read the sign before they've driven past it. Be careful not to over-inflate the balloons. When the signs are loaded in the back of the truck, over-inflated balloons will pop.

The 40 signs will take about two hours for one person to place. However, once the first sign goes up, people will begin arriving at the Open House. Make sure volunteers are in place at the house prepared to sell tickets once the signs start getting placed.

For every Open House use the same signs, and always use red balloons. Red means stop, and it will grab people's attention. People will also begin to associate these signs with the house raffle. Don't print your signs in all caps; this only makes it more difficult to read; and having the signs printed at a sign shop is a waste of money. You'll get more traffic from hand-printed signs. Figure 6 shows the Open House signs.

Kris Harden Photography.

Figure 8. Photo Open House Signs

In the following section I show you how to prepare the home for ticket sales and create an opportunity for the charity to make a good impression on the community and promote its cause. At least two people should run the Open House.

At the Prize Home

Place at least one of the signs in front of the prize home, tie additional red balloons to the house or bushes and trees; and string a banner or large sign that reads In Support of (name of charity) with the charity's logo. Also hang the string of pendent flags (purchased earlier) across the front of the house.

Next, set up a staging area in front of the home outside the front door. If there is a front porch, this is perfect. If not, a canvas-covered canopy will work. What you want to do is introduce the raffle and sell the tickets at this staging spot. If it's too cold or windy to be outside, then set up inside the home near the front entrance.

At the staging area have one or two tables with folding chairs for purchasing tickets. You'll also need these items.

- Blank entry forms

- General fliers about the house raffle (see Appendix K)

- Copies of the Raffle Rules and Restrictions

- A receipt book for cash buys

- A container to hold the completed entry forms

- A manual or electronic credit card machine

- Paper clips to attach checks and credit card slips to the completed entry forms

- Pens and more pens

Wear a fanny pack to hold the cash; never leave money and materials unattended. Finally, post a large sign in the staging area that reads: We accept Checks, Credit Cards, or Cash. If holding cash is unsafe in your area, then only take credit cards and checks at the Open House.

Set out a few extra folding chairs and set clipboards on these chairs holding a stack of entry forms. Attach a pen to each clipboard with a string. This will offer the opportunity for ticket buyers to complete the form while they wait for the volunteers to process payments from others at the tables.

Inside the Prize Home

Inside the house prominently place a large chart on an easel approximately 2 ' x 4 ' with the basics of your house raffle. The easel can be made in advance with two pieces of plywood, and then staple poster-board to the plywood; or purchase an easel at an office supply store. On the chart write a message as such:

Win This Beautiful Home
Or choose $100,000.00 CASH
Benefiting: AAA Best Charity
Only $100 per ticket
Only 4,000 tickets will be sold!
Drawing is November 15

In another area of the home, hang a chart or place several 8.5" x 11" picture frames in which the work of the charity is displayed. From an office supply or craft store you can purchase plastic stand-alone frames that allow you to insert a page. My charity was an animal shelter; so we placed pictures of rescued dogs and cats, along with their story, on tables and counters in every room. Your goal is to visually explain your charity's good work.

So Here It Goes!

People park and walk up to the home and inquire, "A house for $100—what's the catch?"

"To raise funds for disabled children, AAA Best Charity is raffling off this four-bedroom home for $100."

"Oh really!"

"Please take a tour of the home and let me know what you think."

Don't elaborate on the raffle details—they're not ready to hear rules and regulations yet. This statement will be enough information to get them to walk through the home. And don't follow people through the house—stay in the staging area. If they hesitate to enter, then point out a feature about the home. You might say, "It's a four bedroom on a third of an acre, and there's a beautiful brick fireplace in the living room—you're welcome to take a tour."

Most people walk into the home skeptical, but walk out of the home amazed. The home is beautiful, and it's a wonderful prize for only $100. People like the work of the charity and will now want to know more about the raffle details. Don't overwhelm people with information, but do answer all of their questions. Mention that full information is in the Raffle Rules and Restrictions that each ticket buyer will take home. Again, be sure that the person answering the public's questions is well informed about the raffle details and the prize home—be sure that person thoroughly understands the Raffle Rules and Restrictions.

Remember that the IRS has declared that raffle purchases for valuable prizes are not tax-deductible contributions. The buyer is purchasing a chance to win and not simply donating the money. This IRS law is noted in the Raffle Rules and Restrictions. Nevertheless, ticket buyers will want to use this as a tax deduction because it makes them feel better about risking the amount of the raffle ticket; however, not being able to deduct the ticket purchase amount will not stop them from purchasing a ticket. They'll snarl at the IRS and still buy a ticket because they understand that it is not the homeowner or the charity who has come-up with this rule.

Now you can sell the Open House visitor a ticket. When you're handed a credit card ask, "How many tickets would you like?" Don't assume the buyer wants only one. At our raffle, one young lady purchased 10!

Ticket buyers will complete the entry form, provide payment, and leave with either a receipt for cash payment, or a copy of their credit card payment, and a copy of the Raffle Rules and Restrictions (payments by check require no receipt). Once their payment is processed by the charity, a ticket confirmation is sent to them. Remember that the official ticket is kept to be placed in the raffle container for the drawing.

Some people will have questions about the prize home, so those running the open house should know the basics, such as the square footage, lot size, type of heating and cooling, age of the home, and the school district. Surprisingly, some people may want to turn on the shower and check the water pressure or climb in the attic and examine the insulation. Remind them that the house will come with a home warranty. For insurance purposes, don't let people climb in the attic or on the roof. Ask that parents keep their children with them.

Before Visitors Leave

Before visitors leave, ask them to pass the word to neighbors, friends, or co-workers and hand them a flier. Some people will offer to take multiple copies of the flier to distribute at work—that's great, let them. People will want to help so that all the tickets get sold and they get the opportunity to win this fabulous prize. People also like to help a worthy cause—the more community involvement, the better.

If someone does not buy a ticket, give that person a flier in case he/she would like to buy at a later date. Don't give the flier out to people until they are leaving; otherwise, they'll take a flier from the staging area and return to their cars. Your primary goal is to have them tour the house and buy tickets that day.

One common question is: How long will you be selling tickets?

Tell them, "We'll stop selling tickets when we reach 4,000, and we can't predict when we'll be out of tickets."

Don't tell people it would be okay for them to wait a week or more to get their ticket: you really don't know when some big ticket-buyer might swoop in and buy a block of tickets or how rapidly tickets may sell online or at other ticket sale locations. You want people to buy on the spot. Be careful not to pressure them, but don't give them reasons to wait. The time to buy is right now!

Closing Up the Open House

At the end of the day pick up all the signs and store everything in the home for another Open House day. If you hold another Open House in a week, most of the balloons will remain inflated without needing to be replaced. If you sold about 75 - 100 tickets, you had a great day. Be of good cheer! There will be many residuals from your work from people who saw the signs, or heard or read your advertisements, resulting in their coming the next time you stage another Open House. You'll also find people who took fliers will pass the word to others, or buy later. Expect to see your online ticket sales climb after an Open House.

At your next Open House, some ticket buyers will return to measure where they plan to place their furniture or to plant a good-luck charm in the backyard—let them. Also, don't be surprised to see people who didn't buy during the first Open House return in a rush with hopes that there still are tickets left. And don't be surprised to see people who did buy today return with their relatives so that they can buy tickets also.

▶ Marketing requires exposure.
Some people buy after one exposure
while others need several exposures
before making their decision to buy.

Preparing for the Drawing

T his step explains how to address ticket buyers' concerns regarding the raffle, where to hold the drawing, and the helpers and items needed.

Address Their Concerns

There are two main issues ticket buyers are concerned about with a raffle: First, is my ticket number really in the pot? Second, is the person drawing the ticket honest and randomly drawing the ticket? There are several ways to meet both of these concerns and the charity can determine the best means for confirming the integrity of the drawing. The following solutions address the issue of making sure every purchased ticket number is represented in the drawing container. Star ratings are included.

- A CPA firm can perform an audit to verify that all ticket numbers of purchased tickets are included. Their report is then made available to the public upon request. Find out how much time the CPA firm will need so that this can be accomplished before your drawing date. * * * * *

- The tickets can be placed into the drum in the public's view while being filmed. This will take about 3 seconds per ticket and must be scheduled at the drawing site immediately preceding the drawing. Any member of the public wishing to witness this can be present. *Announce this in the media and include the start time in your Raffle Rules and Restrictions.* Use four helpers—one to film and three to take turns watching and placing the tickets into the drum in sequential order. In other words, remove ticket number 1 from the stack and drop it into the drum, then the next numbered ticket and so on, counting aloud as two of the three helpers watch. Every 50 tickets switch helpers. Of course, be sure these helpers have not purchased a ticket. * * * * *

- A reverse drawing can be held so that every single ticket is drawn with the ticket number announced and logged for all to see. At the end, the final remaining ticket numbers are the winners. This will take about 4 seconds per ticket. Due to the time involved and the fact that many people may leave once their ticket is drawn, this is a less positive choice. * * * *

- An employee of the charity can place all tickets in the drum and sign an affidavit that every ticket number was placed in the drum. Remember that charity employees and their immediate family members are excluded from purchasing a raffle ticket. * * *

To address the second concern of the ticket buyer regarding the person drawing the winning tickets, I recommend that the charity use a well-known, local celebrity to draw the winning tickets. Some ideas for celebrities are local weather reporters or news anchors, a local sports figure, the mayor or governor, or a retired movie or sport celebrity living in the area. Again, verify that the celebrity you choose has not purchased a ticket.

Finding a Drawing Location

Think about your public. If you plan to have several Open Houses, then people within driving distance will most likely want to come to the drawing and the raffle drawing will be widely attended. The reason for that is that people who actually entered the home will develop an emotional attachment to the house and their interest will be higher. You'll see. Plus, if you have a popular celebrity drawing the winning tickets, that factor will affect the number of people who will attend. So make sure you have adequate meeting space and parking.

Some ideas for the drawing location are a church hall or community center, the parking lot of a sponsor company, a public park (check city restrictions), or the backyard of the prize home. It isn't necessary to provide seating as the drawing will not take long. Basically, you'll thank the sponsors, the volunteers, and everyone who purchased a ticket. Then you should explain the drawing process, draw the tickets, and congratulate the winners.

Now that the decision is made on how best to cover the ticket buyer's two main concerns and you've chosen a location, you're ready to learn about the helpers and the items needed for the drawing.

Helpers Needed

Arrange for the following helpers in advance and explain their responsibilities.

- A charity employee to locate the winners on the raffle ticket log sheets and to be sure the log sheets are not left unattended.

- Two volunteers to oversee the drawing. Check their identity by viewing their driver's license, and then verify that they are not on the list of ticket buyers. Also, pick people that are not affiliated with each other in any way.

- A celebrity to draw the winning tickets.

On the day of the drawing review the entire drawing procedure with your helpers. The next chapter outlines this procedure, and it's best to explain it to your helpers on the day of the event so it's fresh on their minds.

Items Needed

Gather the following items for the drawing.

- A drum to hold the tickets.

- Tickets numbered 1 – XXX.

- The log sheets in numerical order for the raffle tickets. If it's feasible, consider setting up a computer to access records.

- A loud speaker.

- Two 3" x 5" cards per prize winner. One set will be for the winners and the other set will be labeled for the corresponding runner-ups. For example, Grand Prize, Cash Prize $1,000, etc., are for the winners, and for the runner-ups, First Runner-up, Second Runner-up, etc. (If you have six prizes, have six runner-ups).

- Large manila envelope to hold all the 3" x 5" cards.

- Two permanent ink pens.

- White-board or easel flip chart.

- Felt-tip marking pens.

- A paper stapler.

- A telephone with a speaker function.

- Create a stage so the celebrity is elevated for the crowd to see. If ticket buyers attending the drawing can't see, they will not be happy. Remember, the charity has now started a relationship with these people, and they may become part of their support network for the future.

- Decorations or other items to make the raffle drawing festive. Helium-filled balloons for the kids are a nice gesture. This can be a wonderful opportunity for the charity to further promote their cause to the public so they can make this event as elaborate or as simple as they choose.

- A current fair market evaluation of the prize home completed a few days prior to the drawing. If possible, use the same real estate company that provided the first evaluation when you were setting your home sale price in STEP 3. The charity will need this evaluation for its records, and a copy should be given to the Grand Prize Winner as well.

The IRS will tax the winner based on the current fair market value, and the charity will need to withhold the correct amount. This is not an appraisal that banks use to determine the amount of money to loan on a property. This is a fair market value from a real estate company as if it was listing the property for sale. The charity should use the mid-range price of comparable sales (comps). That is, use the actual sold prices. You must compare to what buyers have actually paid for similar properties in the last 60 days.

The charity may want to hire an appraiser although real estate agents and investors know that there are different conditions that affect the valuation in a formal appraisal. One condition is when you refinance, another is when you apply for an equity line of credit, a third is when you apply for a new mortgage, and a fourth is when determining the value as part of an estate inheritance.

Confusing, but it's true. The same home can receive a different appraised value depending on the purpose for the appraisal. Most people do not pay for an appraisal when they prepare to sell; they get a fair market evaluation by a real estate agent. Verify that your state does not have a law regarding house raffles. If your state does not require a formal appraisal, then use the Fair Market Value provided by one or two real estate agents in your area.

The IRS defines the Fair Market Value as the price at which the property would change hands between a willing buyer and a willing seller, neither being under any compulsion to buy or to sell and both having reasonable knowledge of relevant facts. And the fair market value cannot be determined in a market other than that in which it is most commonly sold to the public, taking into account the location of the property.

Explain to the real estate agent that this home is offered as the prize in a house raffle to benefit the charity, and you want a thorough fair market evaluation of the property for tax reasons. Most agents will do this at no cost because they would like to be considered as the listing agent in the event that the winner decides to put the house on the market; or an agent may do this at no cost for the benefit of the charity.

Game and Bingo supply stores will rent a drum to hold the tickets. Pick a drum larger than the amount of space the tickets will fill. You want to have room for the tickets to circulate about as the drum is turned and not sit there in a clog. Again, ticket buyers are watching and they want to see the tickets moving. This allows them to feel that their tickets are switching places continuously for a better chance to win.

You might contact a party store and ask the store manager to donate the decorations for the raffle drawing event. Tell the store manager that the store can display a banner with their name and logo at the site after the phrase "Decorations provided by. . ." Explain to the store manager that the drawing will be televised, thus providing free advertising for the store. The party store will need some lead-time, so make this request at least 30 days before the drawing date.

The charity should inform the local TV and Radio networks for some free media coverage of the event and send out a press release at least one week before the drawing day. This provides added exposure for the charity, and with the event televised, the odds of someone falsely claiming that the drawing was "fixed" are greatly reduced. You definitely want a public drawing with as many viewers as possible and some states raffle laws require a public drawing. When my house was raffled, over 400 people attended the drawing. One television network filmed the drawing, and the following day, a second network interviewed and filmed the winner at the prize home.

Holding the Drawing

A time of celebration!!! Whoopee, your charity is getting a nice chunk of cash and you're getting your house sold! Not so fast, the drawing is a critical step in the raffle process. If you hold a sloppy drawing, it provides the opportunity for an unhappy ticket buyer, whose ticket number was not drawn, to think the drawing was not done properly. If complaints come in, your funds could be tied up for months through an investigation by the state attorney general. So take extra precautions to hold an organized and fair drawing.

This step explains the announcements to be made before the drawing, the drawing procedure, and notification of the winners. Before you begin, take the time to review the entire drawing procedure with your helpers for the day—the charity employee, the celebrity, and the two overseers.

Announcements

A charity spokesperson should explain the following information to the raffle attendees. Make sure your emcee is briefed in advance, and has printed notes for reference.

The spokesperson should thank everyone for their support, name all sponsors and volunteers who helped make the raffle happen. Explain whatever method the charity chose to safeguard the integrity of the drawing. For example, if the charity chose a CPA, state the name of the firm and that an audit report is available upon request.

Remind attendees that the Grand Prize winner may choose the house or the cash. Tell them that in the event the winner chooses the cash, the home will be listed at a rock-bottom price for a quick sale. Anyone interested should check the charity's website approximately 30 days after the drawing.

The spokesperson needs to explain to people that runner-up tickets (one per winner) will be drawn in the event that the winners do not claim their prizes within 30 days; or are disqualified because they are under age, don't have a Social Security number; or are disqualified for any other reason.

This may seem like over-kill by drawing so many runner-ups, but too many are not a problem. Not having enough is a huge problem, because you will have to give notice to ticket buyers and hold another public drawing for your Grand Prize. So draw one runner-up for each winner and you're safe. Some house raffles include in their rules that the home is donated to the charity if the grand prize winner is disqualified. I don't recommend this method because if the prize is not awarded, it could lead to many complaints and unhappy ticket buyers.

The spokesperson should remind people that the Raffle Rules and Restrictions state that Board members, or employees of (name of charity), employees and agents of the homeowner (name of homeowner) and immediate family members of any of the above are not eligible to participate in this drawing and any tickets purchased by such and or entities will be void. Entrants must also be 18 years or older and have a valid Social Security number.

Finally, the spokesperson should introduce the overseers and the charity employee designated to locate the winners on the log sheets, and then explain the following three points of the drawing process to the public:

1. All winning tickets starting with the Grand Prize winner, down to the lowest cash prize will be drawn and immediately stapled to the 3" x 5" card labeled for that prize and then handed to an overseer. (Hold up the labeled cards for the public to see).

2. Then all runner-up tickets will be drawn and immediately stapled to the cards starting with First Runner-Up, Second Runner-Up, and so on.

3. In the event that a winner is disqualified or doesn't claim the prize, the winner of the prize below them will move up, and the first runner-up

will move into the lowest prize position and so forth. For example, if the Grand Prize winner is disqualified, the winner of the highest cash prize will become the Grand Prize winner, and every winner will move up, also. In this way, the First Runner-up will move into the position of the lowest cash prize. (Outline this on your white-board or flip-chart—some people need a visual).

Grand Prize Winner: **Disqualified**	■1st Place becomes Grand Prize Winner
1st Place Winner: Qualified	
2nd Place Winner: Qualified	■2nd Place becomes 1st Place Winner
3rd Place Winner: Qualified	
4th Place Winner: Qualified	■3rd Place becomes 2nd Place Winner
5th Place Winner: Qualified	
	■4th Place becomes 3rd Place Winner
	■5th Place becomes 4th Place Winner
	■1st Runner-Up is now the 5th Place Winner

Figure 9. Sample Runner-up Visual Display

Note: Do not draw any runner-up tickets until tickets for *ALL* prizes have been drawn. If you draw runner-ups sooner, this will remove them from the chance of winning a prize, and they won't be happy because you have just removed their opportunity to win. Unhappy people complain, and complaints can lead to investigations. You want to be squeaky clean and do this right.

▶ Raffle regulations require that
all ticket buyers have the same
opportunity to win.

Now the spokesperson should introduce the celebrity who will draw the tickets. The celebrity will do the fun part of bantering with the audience and say a few words to the public before actually drawing the tickets. The celebrity might thank the charity for its contribution to the community, and one thing I believe is important to say is that everyone who purchased a raffle ticket is a winner regardless of whose ticket is drawn today because everyone participated in helping a worthy cause. A raffle drawing is a happy and sad event; the winners are "over-the-moon" and the non-winners are disappointed.

> ▶ When you look out at the faces of
> all those ticket holders anticipating the "big win"
> don't be surprised if you find yourself wishing
> that you had 100 homes to give away—I did.

The Drawing Procedure

Do the following steps in the order given to ensure a smooth drawing. It's a good idea for the celebrity to announce the following actions as each one is done.

1. The celebrity draws the Grand Prize ticket, staples it to the 3" x 5" card labeled "GRAND PRIZE" (making sure the ticket number faces outward), and then hands the card to Overseer #1. The same process continues for all prizes in order of highest to lowest, and then from first runner-up to last runner-up.

2. Overseer #1 makes sure that the celebrity has stapled the ticket to the correctly labeled 3" x 5" card. The overseer writes the ticket number on the card, (using a permanent ink pen) and hands the card to the charity employee with the raffle ticket log sheets.

3. The charity employee looks up the names of ticket buyers on the raffle log sheet. The employee then prints the name of the winner on the 3" x 5" card that has the ticket stapled to it.

4. Overseer #2 verifies that the winning name and ticket number on the log sheet match the ticket number written on the card and the number

on the ticket. In other words, Overseer #2 checks everything done by previous handlers.

5. Overseer #2 hands all 3" x 5" cards to the celebrity in the order of last runner-up to first runner-up, and from lowest cash prize winner all the way to Grand Prize winner.

6. The celebrity then announces the winners from bottom to top. For instance, if you have six winners and runner-ups, then it would be:

   A. Ticket number and name of the sixth runner-up. Then the ticket number and name of fifth runner-up, and so on to first runner-up.

   B. Ticket number and name of the sixth lowest cash prize, then the fifth lowest cash prize, and so on to the highest cash prize. If the winners are at the drawing, ask that they come forward to be congratulated and remain up front.

   C. Finally, announce the ticket number and name of the Grand Prize winner and ask the winner to come forward.

It's important to announce your winners in this order so the public will remain until the Grand Prize winner is announced. You want the public to remain until the end because they are your witnesses that the drawing was done "fair and square." Plus, if people are trying to leave in the middle of the drawing, it will be difficult for those remaining to view and hear.

7. Place all 3" x 5" runner-up cards in the manila envelope and seal it. Ask the celebrity to use your permanent ink pen and sign over the seal. Do this in the public's view. Mention to the public that the envelope will be opened only if a winner is disqualified or does not claim the prize.

Notifying the Winners

If the winners are present at the drawing, provide them with a Certificate of Winning and an instruction sheet which informs them of the steps necessary to claim the prize, including the documentation they need to bring to the Claim

Your Prize Appointment. (Samples of the certificate and instructions can be found in Appendices M and N).

If the Grand Prize winner is not present, a fun thing to do is to have the celebrity call the winner on speaker phone with the audience listening. Along with congratulating the winner by phone, notify the winner that the instructions for claiming the prize, along with the certificate of winning, will be mailed within 72 hours.

Although this is not required in the Raffle Rules and Restrictions, I recommend that within 24 hours of the drawing, all winners not present at the drawing be notified by the charity using the telephone numbers provided on the entry form. If there is no answer when called, leaving a message is sufficient. Then within 72 hours, the charity must mail the Certificate of Winning along with the Winner Instruction Sheet for claiming the prize. Mail these by certified mail with a return receipt. This stipulation conforms to the Raffle Rules and Restrictions provided to each ticket buyer. Ticket buyers have 30 days to claim their prize, so inform them immediately so they have as much time as possible to respond.

Note: The procedure for holding the drawing, described in this chapter, is the same procedure that was followed when my house was raffled. I created this drawing procedure in order to carefully complete an organized and fair drawing, avoid any problems, satisfy the ticket buyers concerns, and comply with standard raffle regulations although such regulations are typically general rather than specific. For example, the drawing must be a public drawing, all tickets must be represented in the drawing container, all tickets must have an equal chance of winning, and the winning tickets must be randomly selected. There may be other ways to accomplish the same goals, and the charity may choose to follow a different drawing procedure as long as it complies with any state requirements and it adheres to the Raffle Rules and Restrictions provided to ticket buyers.

Claim-Your-Prize Appointment

T his step describes the paperwork to be completed at the meeting and the tax information required to satisfy the IRS.

If at all possible, the claim-your-prize appointments should be conducted at the prize home. This allows the Grand Prize winner the opportunity to view the home again while deciding whether to take the cash or the home. Although the charity is awarding the prize, it is a good idea for the home seller to attend this meeting in order to answer any questions that may come up about the property. Schedule the appointments with the winners 20 minutes apart with the Grand Prize winner as your last appointment.

Paperwork

At each meeting, the charity director, charity employee, or a charity board member verifies the winner's identity, age, and Social Security number; and the winner signs an affidavit of eligibility stating he or she is not an employee or immediate family member of the charity or the homeowner. (A sample of a Winner Affidavit of Eligibility can be found in Appendix O). Each winner receives the Certificate of Winning if perhaps that person didn't receive it at the time of the drawing.

The Grand Prize winner receives a copy of the current fair market evaluation of the property and a copy of the Property Disclosure Statement—these two documents were supplied earlier to the charity by the homeowner. The Grand Prize winner signs a Prize Acceptance Statement indicating the chosen prize—the house or the cash. (A sample Grand Prize Acceptance Statement can be found in Appendix R).

For tax purposes, all winners must complete Form 5754 which the charity then uses to complete IRS Form W-2G. If the Grand Prize winner chooses the prize home, then the charity will be required to withhold a percentage of the fair market value of the home less the cost of the ticket. If the Grand Prize winner chooses the cash, then the charity will be required to withhold a percentage of the cash amount less the cost of the ticket. Form 5754 can be obtained online at www.irs.gov or from a certified public accountant. The charity must keep Form 5754 for four years and make it available for IRS inspection. (See specific instructions for Form 5754 for more information).

Not all cash prizes require tax withholding; verify the current IRS limits on the IRS website and by consulting a certified public accountant. At the time of my house raffle, the tax withholding applied to winnings of more than $5,000.

The Charity is strongly advised to seek the direction of a certified public accountant for properly withholding the correct percentage amount and filing the appropriate IRS forms required for the year in which the raffle is held.

Additional information may be obtained at Department of the Treasury, IRS website www.irs.gov (see Appendix Q for the IRS Tax withholding notice for tax-exempt organizations and raffle prizes and the Resource section for additional online sites).

Coming Up With That Tax Money

Most lending institutions will accept the Certificate of Winning, along with the lender's appraisal of the home, as sufficient in order to provide the winner with a pre-approval letter for the tax withholding amount since the value of the property is significantly higher than the tax amount. This may be in the form of a home equity line of credit or a mortgage on the property.

For some reason, if the Grand Prize Winner does not qualify for this loan and is unable to provide the required withholding amount (approximately 25% or 28%) for the prize home, the winner will be awarded the cash prize instead as stated in the Raffle Rules and Restrictions.

At the raffle of my home, the charity's CPA determined that there was precedence set for both 25% and 28%, so to reduce the charity's tax liability, they withheld the 28% knowing that if the IRS determines 25% is the correct amount, then when the winner files a tax return for that year, the winner will receive a refund from the IRS.

It's imperative to understand that the exempt organization will be responsible for paying regular gambling withholding or backup withholding whether or not it collects the withholding from the prize recipient.

▶ The best time to collect withholding
or backup withholding is *before* the prize is paid.

Purchase Agreement for the Grand Prize

If the Grand Prize winner chooses the home and can provide the tax withholding amount, then a Purchase Agreement between the charity and the winner is signed. Use the same style form executed between the charity and the home seller. This time the charity is the Seller, and the winner is the Buyer. The Purchase Agreement contains the following elements:

- Purchase price of the home is zero.

- Charity pays any closing costs for the winner from the raffle proceeds if necessary. I believe if the winner does not have to pay closing costs, this will promote more ticket sales, so I recommend that the winner *not* have to incur any additional expenses except for the IRS taxes which are nonnegotiable. The amount of the closing costs can just be part of the expenses for the raffle. (Comply with any state raffle laws).

- There are no inspections. The charity gives the winner the Home Warranty provided by the homeowner. Inspections were previously completed by the warranty company in order to provide a warranty. If the Grand Prize winner wants more inspections done prior to choosing the prize, then that could be accommodated, provided the winner pays for the cost of the inspections.

- Attach an addendum that states the Purchase Agreement is contingent upon the Buyer (Grand Prize winner) providing the tax withholding amount by certified funds on or before the closing date. An example of such an addendum can be found in Appendix P.

Awarding the Prizes

T he charity is responsible to award the raffle prizes. It must award prizes only after every prize winner meets the required qualifications. The reason for this is that just one disqualified winning ticket owner requires moving the next ticket drawn into that spot, bringing other ticket holders up one position, as well.

Then notify the runner-ups that they did not win. Inform them in writing. A nice gesture is to include a gift certificate to a local restaurant to the runner-ups. Remember, the charity is building relationships with all these ticket buyers for the future. The charity may be able to obtain these gift certificates at no cost from a local restaurant.

If you recall, ticket buyers were allowed to purchase a ticket and put a different name on the entry form. The winner is the name on the entry form and that person must meet the requirements to qualify. In the case of the Grand Prize winner, if that individual wants to award the prize home to a minor, the winner can sign over a deed of the property to whomever they choose after taking possession of the house.

When the Grand Prize Winner Takes the Prize Home

There are two Purchase Agreements. The first Purchase Agreement outlines the transfer of the prize home from the home seller to the charity. This Purchase Agreement was signed prior to the beginning of the raffle. The second Purchase Agreement outlines the transfer of the prize home from the charity to the Grand Prize winner. This Purchase Agreement was signed at the claim-your-prize appointment.

Now it's time to set up the closing of the real estate sale. A closing is simply when Buyer and Seller sign the final paperwork that assigns the interest in the property to the new Buyer, and for the Seller to collect a check from the Buyer. As I previously mentioned, I've used a title company in my closing instructions. Once the office handling the closing receives the purchase agreement, that office takes over and prepares the documentation for closing.

Unless your state does not allow for this, ask for a simultaneous closing because you have two closings. The charity purchases from the home seller, thus becoming the new owner. Then the charity transfers title to the Grand Prize winner.

Complete the following items when the winner chooses the prize home:

- The home seller provides copies of both Purchase Agreements to the title company. Explain that you want a simultaneous closing. The title company will begin the paper process of closing the sale and transferring title.

- The home seller schedules an inspection to get the Home Warranty.

- The title company, prior to the settlement signing date, will provide a settlement statement outlining the credits and debits for both parties. The Department of Housing and Urban Development (HUD) has created a standardized closing statement that is used throughout the United States.

- The title company gives a copy of the settlement statement to the escrow company that was holding the raffle funds. The escrow company provides certified funds (to the title company) to cover the closing costs paid by the charity for the Grand Prize winner, and the payout amount required to pay the home seller for the home.

- The home seller brings the following items to the office of the title company at closing: Home Warranty made out in the name of the Grand Prize winner, any closing costs (per settlement statement), all keys, and garage door openers (if applicable). In most cases, the closing costs will come directly out of the sale proceeds; but in the event that there are not sufficient funds to cover them, then the home seller will be required to bring funds to closing. One example might be that there was not enough equity in the home to cover past-due property taxes or late fees to the mortgage company; therefore, the payout amount to the home seller will not cover these costs.

- The winners provide completed Form 5754 *(Statement by Person(s) Receiving Gambling Winnings)* to the charity if it was not provided at the claim-your-prize appointment. The charity will use the information provided on Form 5754 to file Forms W-2G. (See specific instructions for Form 5754 for more information). The charity consults with a certified public accountant for advice and direction on current IRS law.

- The escrow holding company provides payment to the home seller for any agreed-upon compensation (for working on the raffle) listed on the Win-a-House Raffle Agreement. There is no tax withholding amount because the home seller did not win this money—the money was earned.

- At closing the Grand Prize winner is required to provide certified funds (made payable to the charity) for the required withholding tax based on the value of the prize home.

- The escrow holding company provides funds so the charity can award the prize money to the additional prize winners *less any tax withholding amount.* Prize money should be awarded by certified funds.

Unless your individual state has a raffle law to the contrary, the current fair market value of the home should not affect the home's sale price because you are not selling your home to the charity now; you sold it approximately 6 months ago when you signed the purchase agreement before the first raffle ticket was sold. You've had your home off the market this entire time while you continued to pay holding costs as you allowed the charity the time to raise funds through ticket sales.

▶ If the market dropped,
you are not reducing your price.
If the market climbed,
you are not raising your price.

If the Grand Prize winner does not obtain the tax withholding funds, *both closings* must be rescheduled, or the winner may be awarded the cash prize option.

After the successful closing of both real estate sales, you now have a check for the sale of your home, and the winner has a deed to the prize home. Don't forget to transfer the utilities out of your name.

When the Grand Prize Winner Takes the Cash

Complete the following items:

- The home seller provides a copy of the Purchase Agreement to the title company. The title company will begin the paper process of closing the sale and transferring title to the charity.

- The home seller schedules an inspection to get the Home Warranty.

- The title company, prior to the settlement signing date, will provide the HUD settlement statement outlining the credits and debits for both parties.

- The title company gives a copy of the settlement statement to the escrow company holding the raffle funds. The escrow company provides certified funds (to the title company) to cover the payout amount required to pay the home seller for the home.

- The home seller brings the following items to the office of the title company at closing: Home Warranty made out in the name of the charity, any closing costs (per settlement statement), all keys, and garage door openers (if applicable).

- The winners provide completed Form 5754 *(Statement by Person(s) Receiving Gambling Winnings)* to the charity if it was not provided at the claim-your-prize appointment. The charity will use the information provided on Form 5754 to file Forms W-2G. (See specific instructions for Form 5754 for more information). The charity consults with a certified public accountant for advice and direction on current IRS law.

- The escrow holding company provides payment to the home seller for any agreed-upon compensation (for working on the raffle) listed on the Win-a-House Raffle Agreement. There is no tax withholding amount because the home seller did not win this money—the money was earned.

- The escrow holding company provides funds so the charity can award the prize money to the prize winners *less the tax withholding amount.* Prize money should be awarded by certified funds.

Note: If the charity elected not to own the property, then follow the holding fee agreement executed prior to the start of the raffle in which the home seller retains title if the grand prize winner chooses the cash option as the prize.

When Prize Winners Are Disqualified or Fail to Claim the Prize

If any winner is disqualified or fails to claim the prize within the allotted 30 days, the charity should inform the individual in writing. Sending the letter does not provide the winner additional time to respond if the person has missed the deadline; it merely notifies the individual that the prize will be awarded to the owner of the next ticket drawn.

In compliance with the Raffle Rules and Restrictions, in the unlikely event that Grand Prize claimants and runner-ups are exhausted, a new drawing must be scheduled within 10 days and announced in a local newspaper of the charity's choosing. In the unlikely event that you exhaust your list of runner-ups for additional prizes other than the Grand Prize, those unclaimed prizes will be transferred as a donation to the charity.

FINISHED!

Now you can sing!!! Revel in the fact that you stepped outside the box. You sold your house at your asking price, and you provided a wonderful opportunity for a worthy charity to raise funds for its cause. And many lucky winners are celebrating because of your determination. Congratulations!!!

I'm glad I could help.

Diane Giraudo McDermott

APPENDICES

All documents in these appendices are provided as a courtesy. The users of such documents are solely responsible for verifying their legality and accuracy as it applies to their individual situation and the laws and ordinances of their particular city and state. Neither the publisher nor the author assumes any responsibility for any misuse, or any damages caused by their use.

Basics of a House Raffle

1. Raffle tickets are sold to raise funds for the charity and pay for raffle expenses to include the grand prize home.

2. The homeowner and the charity sign a Purchase Agreement for the home with a closing date to take place after the successful completion of the raffle.

3. Ticket buyers purchase a chance to win, so the IRS does not consider the ticket cost to be a charitable donation.

4. All funds coming in from ticket sales are kept in an escrow account.

5. The drawing date may be extended if not enough tickets are sold. The ticket purchasers are notified in writing of an extension.

6. A public drawing is held.

7. The sale of the prize home is closed (completed) between the homeowner and the charity, and the charity and the winner.

8. The charity awards any additional prizes to the winners

9. If the grand prize winner chooses the cash prize, then the charity may, at its discretion, reduce the price of the home for a quick sale.

10. The charity is responsible to withhold taxes from the winner and pay these taxes to the IRS and file appropriate tax forms.

11. The homeowner may merely provide the grand prize, or become actively involved in the raffle process.

12. Raffle Rules and Restrictions apply, and any state or local ordinances must be incorporated.

Fundraising Raffle in support of

_____
(Name of Charity)

Prize:_____ Home, or $_____ Cash

Home Location:_____

Ticket price: $_____

Odds of winning: One in_____

Drawing Date/Time & Location: _____

RAFFLE RULES & RESTRICTIONS

1. _____ is a 501 (c) ( ) _____
       (Name of Charity)   (State)

tax-exempt nonprofit charitable organization. The net proceeds of this raffle will be used to support _____.
                             (Name of Charity)

This raffle is registered with the Office of the _____
                                        (State)

Attorney General, _____ Raffle Registration
                      (state)

Number _____

2. The purchase price of a raffle ticket is $_____. Checks or money orders should be made out to _____.
                             (Name of Charity)

Cash, Money Orders, Visa, Discover, and MasterCard are accepted.

3. The IRS has declared that raffle purchases for valuable prizes are not tax-deductible contributions.

4. Ticket purchases are available in the following ways:

By phone: _____

Fax: _____

Mail to:_____

Online at: _____

In person at the following location(s):

_____

_____

_____

5. In the event an entrant's check or credit card is declined by the bank or credit card company, the entry is declared invalid and withdrawn from the drawing.

6. Entrants must be 18 years or older and have a valid Social Security number to purchase a raffle ticket and be included in the drawing. All prize winners will be required to submit a signed affidavit of eligibility, photo identification, taxpayer identification number, and such written information as is required by any applicable tax and/or real estate laws, including without limitation to their Social Security number, proof of identity in forms acceptable to _____ and other identifying information or they
(Name of Charity)

will be deemed ineligible to claim the prize. Anyone who does not comply will be disqualified and the prize will go to the next ticket drawn.

7. All completed ticket entry forms must be received with full payment no later than 5:00 p.m., (circle) EST, CDT, MST, PDT on _____
(5 days before drawing)

or before a total of _____ tickets are sold, whichever comes first.
_____ has the right to continue selling
(Name of Charity)

tickets, at its discretion, until the scheduled drawing on _____.

8. In the unlikely event that a sufficient number of tickets are not sold by
_____, _____ has the right to
(Drawing Date)   (Name of Charity)

accept less than _____ tickets sold or extend the drawing for up to 60 days by providing written notice to ticket purchasers. Notice may be given by U.S. Mail or by electronic mail.

9. In the unlikely event that a sufficient number of tickets are not sold to ensure a drawing on the scheduled drawing date or after an extended drawing date, then _____ will refund the money collected for raffle
(Name of Charity)

ticket sales within 30 calendar days of the date of raffle cancellation and all prizes will be withdrawn.

10. The Grand Prize is a _____ Bedroom Home located at
_____.

The home is valued at approximately _____; or the winner may choose the alternative grand prize of $_____ cash. Additional prizes are _____
_____.

11. All prizes will be awarded through a random drawing held on _____, at _____ (circle) EST, CDT, MST, PDT
(Date) (Time)
at _____.
(Location)

12. Confirmation that all ticket numbers purchased are placed in the raffle container will be done by _____
_____.

13. The winner need not be present to win. The winner will be notified using the contact information provided on the winning ticket entry form. A notice will be mailed and postmarked within 72 hours of the drawing. The winner's name and winning ticket number will be posted on the _____
(Name of Charity)
web site for 30 days after the drawing.

14. A copy of these rules and restrictions and winners' names and ticket numbers may be requested by sending a self-addressed-stamped envelope to
_____
_____
_____

15. All prizes must be claimed no later than 5:00 p.m. (circle) EST, CTD, MST, PDT on _____. Such date is 30 days from the drawing date. If the prize is not claimed by that date, this will constitute a forfeiture of the prize and the prize will be awarded to the next ticket drawn.

16. Providing notification to_____
(Name of Charity)

in one of the following ways by the date noted in paragraph (15) will constitute Claiming the Prize.

(a) Prize winner delivers a written notice signed by winner to _____ _____ and winner obtains a signed Proof of
(Name of Charity)

Delivery signed by _____.
(Name of Charity Designee)

(b) Prize winner sends written notice by certified mail with return receipt – signature required to: _____
(Name of Charity)

Attention:_____
(Name of Charity Designee)

at_____
(Charity Address)

17. _____will make reasonable effort to contact
(Name of Charity)
the winners using the information completed by the ticket buyer on the raffle entry form. If despite this effort, the winner cannot be located within 30 calendar days after the drawing, or if any such person is ineligible under these Rules and Restrictions or applicable law, then that person will not be awarded the prize, and the prize will go to the next ticket drawn.

18. In the event that all runner-ups have been exhausted to claim the Grand Prize, a new drawing will be scheduled within 10 days. The new drawing date will be announced in _____
(Newspaper)
and at the following website _____

19. In the event that all runner-ups have been exhausted to claim prizes other than the Grand Prize, those unclaimed prizes will be transferred as a donation to _____.
(Name of Charity)

20. In order for the Grand Prize winner to receive the home, the winner must make their decision known that they are choosing the home, instead of the cash prize to _____ by the deadline in paragraph (15).
(Name of Charity)
This notice of prize choice from the winner must be in writing and signed by the winner. If _____ does not
(Name of Charity)
receive an effective notice by this deadline, then the Grand Prize winner will be automatically and irrevocably deemed to have elected not to receive the home and to have elected to receive the Alternate Cash Grand Prize.

21. If the Grand Prize winner provides adequate written decision to receive the home, but is unable to provide the required withholding tax amount, or any such other items as are needed to complete the transfer of the Property, then _____may award the Alternate Cash Grand
(Name of Charity)
Prize instead of the Grand Prize Home.

22. If the home is claimed as the prize, the prize winner will execute a Purchase Agreement for the home with _____.
(Name of Charity)
Winner shall reasonably cooperate in the escrow process and promptly sign and deliver such documents as are customary for acquiring residential real estate.

23. The Internal Revenue Service requires that any prizes valued at $600 or more be issued a W-2G Form. The IRS also requires that 25% or 28% (backup withholding) of the value of the prize be withheld for federal taxes on winnings of more than $5,000. At the time of the drawing, if such IRS laws have changed, the current applicable law will apply.

24. The prize winner is solely responsible for paying and reporting, as required by law all local, state, federal taxes whether or not _____
(Name of Charity)
makes any withholding for taxes from the winning amount, and each winner authorizes the withholding from any prize the amounts required to be withheld by applicable law and shall indemnify, defend, protect and hold harmless _____ against all claims relating to
(Name of Charity)

such taxes and expenses.

25. _____ is not held responsible for any
(Name of Charity)

express or implied warranties in regarding this prize. The prize is offered in "AS IS" condition. A Home Warranty will be provided at the time of Closing, as laid out in the Purchase Agreement and all due property taxes, liens, and mortgages will be paid off at the time of closing, and the winner will receive a free and clear property covered by title insurance.

26. _____ and the Seller of the home do not
(Name of Charity)

make any guarantee, agreement, representation, or warranty as to the value of the home or that the recipient of the home will be able to sell it for any certain price or within any certain time period.

27. _____ or the Seller of the home assume
(Name of Charity)

no liability for lost, late, misdirected, mutilated, incomplete, illegible, or entries without complete payment which will be deemed invalid and disqualified. Nor do they assume any responsibility for notifying anyone who attempts to purchase a raffle ticket without good funds.

28. In the event that more than one name or group of individuals is listed on the winning ticket entry form, the first name listed will be deemed the winner. It is the sole responsibility of the winner to distribute any such prize shares to other participants in the multiple parties listed.

29. Board members, or employees of _____,
(Name of Charity)

employees and agents of _____, and
(Homeowner)

immediate family members of any of the above are not eligible to participate in this drawing and any tickets purchased by such and or entities will be void.

30. The prize winner understands, acknowledges, and agrees that he/she is receiving a prize and will hereby release and discharge _____
_____, the Seller of the home, and any   (Name of Charity)
additional sponsors, their employees, agents, officers, directors, and legal representatives and assigns from any and all claims, liabilities, damages, losses, injuries or expenses arising from or caused by the award of such a prize or as a result of this raffle and/or that person's failure to win or redeem any prize including, but not limited to, the payment of any and all taxes that are due.

31. The Grand Prize winner acknowledges that government authorities may place a different value on the home than _____.

(Name of Charity)

32. The purchase of a raffle ticket constitutes the buyer's acceptance of all rules and restrictions governing this raffle as outlined herein.

33. The decisions of _____ are final on all

(Name of Charity)

matters concerning the raffle.

34. Void where prohibited.

Purchase Agreement Real Estate

1. This Agreement is entered into between *Thomas Homeseller,* herein called Buyer, whose address is: *714 Silver Dr. Pleasant City, New Mexico 00000* and *AA Best Charity* herein called Seller whose address is *3000 Daisy Lane, Pleasant City, New Mexico 00000.* Buyer hereby agrees to purchase and Seller agrees to sell and convey the following described real estate with all improvements, and fixtures, plus the personal Property described herein upon the Terms and Conditions Hereinafter Set Forth.

2. The Real Estate is located in *Beautiful* County, State of *New* Mexico and is described as follows:

(Insert legal description).

> *Lot number 00, Block 0 Mountain View Hills, Unit 00, Superior City Plat Book No. 00, Page 18, 19, 20.*

Address: *714 Silver Dr., Pleasant City, New Mexico 00000*

3. PURCHASE PRICE *$ 250,000.00*

- Cash Down Payment *$None*
- Amount of the Loan: $ *Cash Buy*
- Earnest Money: *$ None* will be delivered by Buyer in the form of ( ) check, ( ) Cash, ( ) Note, dated: _____

Earnest money will be applied to Purchase Price and/or closing costs upon Funding Date. Earnest money to be deposited upon execution of this agreement with _____ (Escrow agent or Title Company).

Buyer CE___ Seller TH___   *Page 1 of 15*

4. Fixtures and Personal Property. Seller agrees to transfer to Buyer free of liens all items attached to the Property unless noted on the list of items excluded from the sale.

The following items are excluded from the sale: *Refrigerator and clothes washer and clothes dryer.*

The following personal items are included in the sale: *None*

5. Time is of the Essence. Buyer and Seller understand that time is of the essence for this Agreement.

6. Rights to Property Ownership. Note the description of any known mineral or water rights appurtenant to the Property and whether they will be included in the sale: *No known water and mineral rights*

MONETARY OBLIGATIONS

7. Appraisal Contingency. It is agreed by both parties that Buyer is not obligated to complete the purchase of the Property if the purchase price exceeds the appraised value completed by a licensed real estate appraiser or the lending institution to which a loan application has been made. If Buyer elects not to proceed with the purchase, then Buyer must provide written notice to Seller of such election within ___2___ business days of receiving the written appraisal. Seller may, at Seller's discretion, reduce the purchase price by delivering written notice to Buyer within 3 days of receipt of the Buyer's written notice. If Seller does not elect to reduce the purchase price, Buyer may proceed with the consummation of this Agreement despite the appraised value, or terminate the Agreement without penalty and all earnest money will be returned to Buyer.

8. (   ) Mortgage Loan. This Agreement is contingent on Buyer obtaining a $___*N/A*___ loan within _____ business days of the date of Acceptance. If Buyer is unable to procure said mortgage and thus provide Seller with written rejection, this Agreement will terminate and earnest money paid by Buyer will be refunded. In the event that Buyer successfully obtains said loan, Buyer must present written acceptance to Seller within the business days noted or Seller may deem that the Buyer was unsuccessful in procuring the loan and Seller may terminate this Agreement and all earnest money must be refunded to Buyer.

9. (   ) Seller Financing. The amount of $ _____*N/A*_____ will be financed by Seller and secured by one of the following:

_____ Real Estate Contract
_____ Mortgage
_____ Deed of Trust

The terms of which are attached to this Agreement as Addendum No. _____

10. (   ) VA Financing. It is agreed by both parties that Buyer is not obligated to complete the purchase of the Property if the purchase price exceeds the reasonable value of the Property confirmed by the Department of Veterans Affairs. If Buyer elects not to proceed with the purchase, then Buyer must provide written notice to Seller of such election within _*N/A*_ business days of receiving the written Property value. Seller may, at Seller's discretion, reduce the purchase price by delivering written notice to Buyer within 3 days of receipt of the Buyer's written notice. If Seller does not elect to reduce the purchase price, Buyer may proceed with the consummation of this Agreement despite the value received from the Department of Veterans Affairs, or terminate the Agreement without penalty and all earnest money will be returned to Buyer.

11. (   ) FHA Financing. It is agreed by both parties that Buyer is not obligated to complete the purchase of the Property if the purchase price exceeds the reasonable value of the Property confirmed by the Fair Housing Commissioner. If Buyer elects not to proceed with the purchase, then Buyer must provide written notice to Seller of such election within _____*N/A*_____ business days of receiving the written Property value. Seller may, at Seller's discretion, reduce the purchase price by delivering written notice to Buyer within 3 days of receipt of the Buyer's written notice. If Seller does not elect to reduce the purchase price, Buyer may proceed with the consummation of this Agreement despite the value received from the Fair Housing Commissioner, or terminate the Agreement without penalty and all earnest money will be returned to Buyer.

12. (*CE***   ) Cash Offer.** The purchase price amount is available to Buyer and Buyer will provide written proof of funds to Seller within ___*N/A*___ days of Acceptance. *See Raffle Contingency Addendum No.1.*

13. Proof of Funds. Buyer agrees to provide written proof of funds to Seller within ___*N/A*___ days from the date of Acceptance. Proof of down payment, and/or proof of the balance of the purchase price are required.

14. Property Disclosures. Seller represents to Buyer that Seller is unaware of any information that materially affect the value of the Property including violations of governmental laws, rules and regulations, other than those Buyer can observe or that are known or have been disclosed to Buyer. Further, Seller represents that square footage is approximate and Seller does not guarantee accuracy.

Seller declares that Buyer is purchasing the Property upon Buyer's own examination and not by reason of any representation made by Seller, except those that may have been made in this Agreement and in the property disclosure statement.

Buyer understands that Seller makes no representations as to the future value of the Property and Seller strongly advises that Buyer verify any and all conditions of the Property and that Buyer should consult their own respective attorney, accountants, or other professions as to the legal and tax effect of this Agreement prior to signing.

15. Home Warranty Contract. If marked in paragraph 17, a home warranty service contract will be purchased from *AAA Home Inspection Company*_____. The Buyer and Seller acknowledge that the home warranty service contract provides limited coverage and may contain specific exclusions and or deductibles. The home warranty company may or may not conduct an inspection of the Property. Any inspection report made available by the provider of the warranty is not meant as a representation of the condition of the Property by the Seller, and is only a report by which the warranty provider uses to determine the conditions under which the Property may be warranted. Seller is not responsible for such home warranty coverage or lack thereof.

16. Inspections and or Surveys. Seller strongly encourages Buyer to employ competent professionals to perform inspections or surveys of all conditions of the Property in order to satisfy any concerns Buyer may have.

(A) If Buyer fails to order an inspection or survey to which Buyer has agreed to pay, then Buyer may not use the failure to receive the document by the delivery deadline as reason to terminate this Agreement.

(B) Objections by Buyer must be provided to Seller in writing along with the inspector's or the surveyor's report by the objection deadline. Buyer may request, in writing, that Seller cure the objection; otherwise Buyer may terminate this Agreement.

(C) If no written objection or termination is received by Seller by the objection deadline, then Buyer will be deemed to have waived the contingency of this Agreement.

(D) Inspection or Survey reports ordered by Seller must be provided to Buyer by delivery deadline. If they are not received by Buyer, Buyer may elect to extend the delivery deadline or terminate this Agreement.

(E) Unless agreed to in writing, the party paying for the inspection or survey will choose the inspection or survey company and will be responsible to order the survey or inspection report. Payment is required for all surveys or inspections performed whether or not the sale of the Property closes.

INSPECTION or SURVEY	BUYER PAYS	SELLER PAYS	DELIVERY DEADLINE	OBJECTION DEADLINE	RESOLUTION DEADLINE
American Land Title Association (ALTA)					
Staked Boundary					
Flood Plain Designation					
Improvement Location Report					
Electrical		*X*	4/19/10	4/21/10	4/23/10
Plumbing		*X*	4/19/10	4/21/10	4/23/10
Heating & Air Conditioning		*X*	4/19/10	4/21/10	4/23/10
Structural		*X*	4/19/10	4/21/10	4/23/10
Roof		*X*	4/19/10	4/21/10	4/23/10
Risk Assessment					
Lead-Based Paint Evaluation					
Radon					
Wood-Destroying Pests	*X*		4/19/10	4/21/10	4/23/10
Dry Rot					
Mold					
Asbestos					
Other:					
Other:					
Other					

Buyer CE   Seller TH

(F) If a resolution of any objections is not resolved by the resolution deadline, then this Agreement will be deemed terminated.

(G) If Seller agrees to cure objections, they must be cured no later than _____10_____ days after the resolution deadline.

(H) Seller agrees to provide Buyer and any inspectors and/or surveyors reasonable access to the Property. The party selecting the inspector will be responsible to pay for any damages that occur to the Property by reason of such inspection or survey.

(I) If Buyer chooses not to have any surveys or inspections, Buyer then waives the right to receive such reports and discharges any claims that may arise due to later findings.

(J) Seller agrees to pay for any repairs required by FHA, VA, a conventional lender, or for repairs under Buyer's objections subject to the maximum cost of: $*500.00*. If the cost exceeds this dollar amount, Buyer and Seller may negotiate a resolution. If no resolution is reached, this Agreement will be deemed terminated.

(K) If this Agreement is terminated subject to the conditions listed in this section titled *Inspections and or Surveys*, the earnest money will be refunded to the Buyer.

17. Costs. Buyer & Seller agree to pay the following items as marked:
B = Buyer   S = Seller   N/A = Not applicable

Loan-Related Charges.

Appraisal Fee (*N/A*)	Appraisal Re-inspection Fee (*N/A*)
Credit Report (*N/A*)	Flood Zone certification (*N/A*)
Loan Assumption/Transfer (*N/A*)	Origination Fee (*N/A*)
Points Buy-down (*N/A*)	Points Discount (*N/A*)
Tax Service Fee (*N/A*)	Underwriting Review Fee (*N/A*)

Loan Documentation Preparation (*N/A*)
Other (*N/A*)
Describe Other: _____

Prepaid Items Required by the Lender.

Hazard Insurance (*N/A*)   Flood Insurance (*N/A*)
Interest (*N/A*)   PMI or MIP (*N/A*)
Taxes (*N/A*)   Other (*N/A*)

Describe Other: _____

Title Company Closing Costs.

Closing Fee (*S*)   Legal Document Preparation (*S*)
Special Assessment Search (*S*) Transfer Fees *(S*)
Recording Fees (*S*)   Other (   )

Describe Other: _____

Policy Premiums.

Title Commitment (*S*)   Standard Owner's Policy (*S*)
Mortgagee's Policy (   )   Survey (   )
Impact Fees (   )   Home Warranty Contract (*S*)
Transfer Fees (*S*)   Other (   )

Describe Other: _____

Escrow Fees.

Set up   (*S*)   Periodic   (   )
Close out (*S*)   Other   (   )

Describe Other: _____

18. Prorated Items. Any and all applicable specific fees regarding the Property, including but not limited to rent or lease payments, general real estate taxes, insurance payments, interest, rents and other expenses and revenue of the Property, and homeowners' association dues will be prorated as of the date of closing. Buyer and Seller will directly handle any contract service agreements. Seller will be responsible for disclosing such contract service agreements to the Buyer.

19. Assessments. All assessments, bonds, and impact fees that are part or paid with the Property tax bill of the Property shall be assumed by Buyer. If other assessments, bonds, and impact fees constitute a lien upon the Property, the current installment will be prorated as of the Closing date, and Buyer shall assume future installments. This Agreement is contingent upon verification and written approval by Buyer and Seller of the amount of all assessments, bonds, and impact fees to be assumed or paid within ten (10) days after receipt of the title commitment approval date. In the event that either party disapproves, such party may terminate this Agreement by giving a written notice to the other party on or before the approval date. Buyer will pay the future assessments for improvements including, but not limited to, sidewalks, driveway cuts or roads.

20. Title and Liens. (   ) Buyer or (X) Seller will order a title commitment. Such title commitment will be ordered from *ABC Title Company*   (title company) within ___*2*___ days after acceptance.   Buyer will have ___*2*___days (objection deadline) to object to title exceptions after receiving the title commitment and all accompanying documents referred to therein. Unless the Buyer provides written objection to the Seller by the objection deadline, any exceptions to the title will be deemed approved.

If Seller is unwilling or unable to remove such exceptions before the Settlement Signing Date, Seller will provide written notice to Buyer within ___*2*___ days after receipt of Buyer's objections. Buyer may choose to close subject to exceptions; remove said exceptions at Buyer's expense; reduce the amount of the purchase price subject to Seller approval; or terminate this Agreement. If Buyer terminates this agreement, the earnest money will be refunded to Buyer.

21. Deed. Conveyance of the Property by ___*Warranty Deed*___ subject only to any items identified in the title commitment and not objected to by Buyer as provided in paragraph 20. The legal description written in the deed will be the same legal description written in the title commitment and any survey obtained under paragraph 16.

22. Insurance Contingency. This agreement is contingent upon Buyer being able to obtain, at normal and customary rates, a homeowner's or property insurance binder on the Property. If Buyer fails to make application for insurance within ___5___ days after date of acceptance of this Agreement, then this contingency will be deemed waived. If Buyer is unable to obtain such a binder for insurance after making a good faith effort and gives timely notice of such inability, then the Purchase Agreement will terminate and the earnest money will be refunded to Buyer.

23. Seller Disclosure. Seller will deliver in writing to Buyer a Seller's Property Disclosure Statement within ___2___ days after date of acceptance of this Agreement. Buyer in turn must deliver to Seller any and all objections in writing as they pertain to the disclosure statement within ___3___ days after having received the Seller's Property Disclosure Statement. The deadline to resolve any objections to the disclosure statement is within ___5___ days of the date Seller receives written objections from Buyer. In the event that a resolution cannot be reached, this Agreement will terminate.

Other documents required from Seller_____

_____

Deadlines and obligations noted in paragraph 23 will apply to any additional document requirements listed.

24. Lead-Based Paint.
(   ) The dwelling was built BEFORE 1978 and as required by federal law, an addendum providing Seller's Disclosure of Lead-Based Paint and Lead-Based Paint Hazards is attached to this Agreement. Seller cannot legally accept this offer to purchase until Buyer has received and had an opportunity to review this addendum.

(*TH*) The dwelling was built in or AFTER 1978. Therefore, Seller is not required to make any disclosure of lead-based paint or lead-based paint hazards.

Buyer CE   Seller TH___   *Page 10 of 15*

25. (   ) Septic System. The Property includes an on-site liquid waste system; therefore, the transfer of the Property may be subject to state regulations governing on-site liquid waste systems. Septic System Contingency Addendum No. _____ is attached.

26. Closing. This Agreement to Purchase shall be closed and the General Warranty Deed or other deed shall be delivered to Buyer on or before _____16_____ day of _November, 2010_. The closing shall take place at the office of _____ABC Title Company_____ (Seller's attorney, Buyer's lender, the Escrow Agent, Title Insurance office or as otherwise agreed upon).

Unless otherwise agreed in writing, failure to close the sale on the closing date shall constitute a default under this Purchase Agreement. Buyer and Seller agree to sign and deliver to the closing officer all documents required to complete the transaction and to perform all other closing obligations for this Agreement on or before the closing date.

Buyer and Seller agree to provide for the delivery of all required certified funds, if any, using wired or other ready funds acceptable to the title company on or before the closing date. In the event of non-payment, the non-performing party may request the other party in writing to extend the closing date. Acceptance of any new closing date must be presented in writing.

27. Possession. Buyer and Seller agree that Seller will give possession of the Property to Buyer by 5 p.m. on: _____ _Day of Closing_____.

28. Condition of Property at time of Possession. Seller agrees to deliver possession of said Property in broom-clean condition, and that all personal property not included in this purchase agreement shall be removed from the Property at Seller's expense before delivery of Property to Buyer. Except for ordinary wear and tear, Seller agrees to deliver Property to Buyer in the same condition as existed on the date of acceptance.

29. Walk-through Prior to Closing. Buyer shall have the right to inspect the Property within two days prior to closing date in order to determine if Property is in the same condition, normal wear and tear excepted, as it was at the time of acceptance.

30. Termite Inspection. Within ___7___ business days from the date of acceptance of this agreement, the Buyer, at Buyer's expense, has the right to obtain an inspection with a written report from a licensed pest control firm as to the evidence of termite or other wood-boring insect infestation on the Property. If infestation exists Buyer has ___2___ business days upon receiving such report, either to proceed with the purchase or to cancel this agreement. Such cancellation must be in writing and delivered to the Seller within the time-frame noted.

31. Flood Hazard Zone. If the Property is located in a special flood hazard area, Buyer may be required to pay flood insurance in order to obtain a loan secured by the Property. In this event, Buyer may elect to cancel this agreement without penalty and the earnest money will be refunded to Buyer.

32. Zoning. The Property must be properly zoned for __*Residential*__ _____ use. No deed restrictions should exist against such use at the time of closing; otherwise, Buyer may choose to terminate this agreement without penalty and the earnest money will be refunded to Buyer. It is Buyer's sole responsibility to adequately verify zoning by contacting the city zoning department or by any other such appropriate means.

33. Entire Agreement. This Purchase Agreement, along with the following addendum(s) and any exhibits referred to in this Purchase Agreement constitute the entire agreement between Buyer and Seller and cannot be amended, changed, or modified in any way except by written agreement of both parties. The Buyer and Seller further understand that this offer, if accepted in writing by Seller and delivered to Buyer, constitutes a legally binding contract.

Addendum No. *1 Re: Raffle Contingency*
Addendum No. *2 Re: Opening escrow holding account for raffle funds*
Lead-Based Paint Addendum No. *3 Re: Disclosure*
Septic System Contingency Addendum No. _____
Real Estate Contract Addendum No. _____
Miscellaneous Addendum No. _____

34. Notice. All notices must be in writing and delivered to the parties at the addresses shown on the signature page of this Purchase Agreement. Notices may be made by U.S. registered or certified mail with return receipt requested, hand-delivered, or sent by facsimile.

35. By Law. All terms and conditions of this Agreement will be governed by the laws of the state of _____*New Mexico*_____ and are subject to the practices of good faith and fair dealing. Seller is responsible to provide to Buyer, at Seller's expense, all certificates of inspection, certificates of occupancy, or any such items as required by any local ordinance.

36. Mediation. If a dispute arises between the parties relating to this agreement, the parties agree to submit the dispute to mediation. Buyer and Seller will jointly appoint a mediator and equally share the costs of the mediation. If Buyer and Seller cannot agree upon the appointment of a mediator, or if there is no resolution reached through mediation, Buyer and Seller may enforce their rights and obligations under this agreement in any manner provided by law in the state governing this agreement.

37. Attorney Fees. If litigation is instituted to require either party to perform the stipulations of this agreement, then the prevailing party is entitled to recover all costs incurred, including but not limited to attorney fees and court costs as ordered by the court.

38. Fair Housing. Buyer and Seller understand that the Fair Housing Act prohibits discrimination in the sale or financing of housing on the basis of race, color, age, religion, sexual orientation, gender identity, familial status, spousal affiliation, physical or mental handicap, serious medical condition, national origin or ancestry.

39. Risk of Loss. Risk of loss or damage to the Property by any reason is retained by the Seller until closing. Buyer may choose to extend the date of closing to allow Seller to restore the Property to its previous condition; accept the Property "as is" with Seller assigning the insurance proceeds to Buyer at closing; or terminate this Agreement with all earnest money refunded to Buyer.

40. Earnest Money Dispute. If Buyer fails to perform, all money paid pursuant to this agreement by Buyer shall be retained by Seller as consideration for the execution of this agreement as agreed liquidated damages, and in full settlement of any claims or damages. If Seller fails to perform due to factors beyond Seller's control, all money paid by Buyer pursuant to this agreement will be returned to Buyer on demand; or Buyer will only have the right of specific performance.

41. Foreign Sellers. The Foreign Investment in Real Property Tax Act (FIRPTA) may apply if Seller is a foreign person, foreign corporation or partnership, or nonresident alien, unless the purchase price is less than $300,000 and the Buyer intends to use the Property as the Buyer's residence. FIRPTA may require that the Buyer of real Property withhold 10 percent of the sale price and to deposit that amount with the IRS at the time of closing.

(   ) Seller is subject to FIRPTA
(*X*) Seller is not subject to FIRPTA

42. Expiration of Offer. This offer will terminate if not accepted before:

April 7 (mo/day), *2010* (year), *5:00 p.m.,* (time), *Mountain Standard Time* (time zone) in writing to Buyer or Buyer's Agent.

Purchase Agreement Signature Page

TIME IS OF THE ESSENCE OF THIS AGREEMENT.

Buyer

Buyer acknowledges that Buyer has read the entire Purchase Agreement and Buyer understands and accepts the terms specified in this agreement.

AAA Best Charity – Charlene Executorship
Print Buyer(s) Name

Charlene Executorship   *April 7, 2010 2:00 p.m.*
Buyer Signature   Date/Time

3000 Daisy Lane, Pleasant City, NM 00000
Buyer Address   E-mail

000-000-0000   *000-000-0000*   *000-000-0000*
Buyer Home phone   Business phone   Fax

Seller

Seller agrees to sell the property at the price and terms specified in this agreement.

Thomas Homeseller
Print Seller(s) Name

Thomas Homeseller   *April 7, 2010 2:05 p.m.*
Seller Signature   Date/Time

714 Silver Dr., Pleasant City, NM 00000
Seller Address   E-mail

000-000-0000   *000-000-0000*   *000-000-0000*
Seller Home phone   Business phone   Fax

Page 15 of 15

Purchase Agreement Real Estate

1. This Agreement is entered into between _____, herein called Buyer, whose address is: _____ and _____ herein called Seller whose address is _____ _____. Buyer hereby agrees to purchase and Seller agrees to sell and convey the following described real estate with all improvements, and fixtures, plus the personal Property described herein upon the Terms and Conditions Hereinafter Set Forth.

2. The Real Estate is located in _____ County, State of _____and is described as follows:

(Insert legal description)

Address: _____

3. PURCHASE PRICE $_____

Cash Down Payment $_____

Amount of the Loan: $_____

Earnest Money: $_____ will be delivered by Buyer in the form of ( ) check, ( ) Cash, ( ) Note, dated: _____

Earnest money will be applied to Purchase Price and/or closing costs upon Funding Date. Earnest money to be deposited upon execution of this agreement with _____ (Escrow agent or Title Company).

Buyer _____ *Seller*_____   *Page 1 of 15*

4. Fixtures and Personal Property. Seller agrees to transfer to Buyer free of liens all items attached to the Property unless noted on the list of items excluded from the sale.

The following items are excluded from the sale: _____
_____
_____

The following personal items are included in the sale: _____
_____

5. Time is of the Essence. Buyer and Seller understand that time is of the essence for this Agreement.

6. Rights to Property Ownership. Note the description of any known mineral or water rights appurtenant to the Property and whether they will be included in the sale: _____
_____

MONETARY OBLIGATIONS

7. Appraisal Contingency. It is agreed by both parties that Buyer is not obligated to complete the purchase of the Property if the purchase price exceeds the appraised value completed by a licensed real estate appraiser or the lending institution to which a loan application has been made. If Buyer elects not to proceed with the purchase, then Buyer must provide written notice to Seller of such election within _____ business days of receiving the written appraisal. Seller may, at Seller's discretion, reduce the purchase price by delivering written notice to Buyer within 3 days of receipt of the Buyer's written notice. If Seller does not elect to reduce the purchase price, Buyer may proceed with the consummation of this Agreement despite the appraised value, or terminate the Agreement without penalty and all earnest money will be returned to Buyer.

8. (   ) Mortgage Loan. This Agreement is contingent on Buyer obtaining a $_____ loan within _____ business days of the date of Acceptance. If Buyer is unable to procure said mortgage and thus provide Seller with written rejection, this Agreement will terminate and earnest money

paid by Buyer will be refunded. In the event that Buyer successfully obtains said loan, Buyer must present written acceptance to Seller within the business days noted or Seller may deem that the
Buyer was unsuccessful in procuring the loan and Seller may terminate this Agreement and all earnest money must be refunded to Buyer.

9. (   ) Seller Financing. The amount of $_____ will be financed by Seller and secured by one of the following:

_____ Real Estate Contract

_____ Mortgage

_____ Deed of Trust

The terms of which are attached to this Agreement as Addendum No. _____

10. (   ) VA Financing. It is agreed by both parties that Buyer is not obligated to complete the purchase of the Property if the purchase price exceeds the reasonable value of the Property confirmed by the Department of Veterans Affairs. If Buyer elects not to proceed with the purchase, then Buyer must provide written notice to Seller of such election within _____ business days of receiving the written Property value. Seller may, at Seller's discretion, reduce the purchase price by delivering written notice to Buyer within 3 days of receipt of the Buyer's written notice. If Seller does not elect to reduce the purchase price, Buyer may proceed with the consummation of this Agreement despite the value received from the Department of Veterans Affairs, or terminate the Agreement without penalty and all earnest money will be returned to Buyer.

11. (   ) FHA Financing. It is agreed by both parties that Buyer is not obligated to complete the purchase of the Property if the purchase price exceeds the reasonable value of the Property confirmed by the Fair Housing Commissioner. If Buyer elects not to proceed with the purchase, then Buyer must provide written notice to Seller of such election within _____ business days of receiving the written Property value. Seller may, at Seller's discretion, reduce the purchase price by delivering written notice to Buyer within 3 days of receipt of the Buyer's written notice. If Seller does not elect to reduce the purchase price, Buyer may proceed with the consummation of this Agreement despite the value received from the Fair Housing Commissioner, or terminate the Agreement without penalty and all earnest money will be returned to Buyer.

Buyer _____ *Seller* _____   *Page 3 of 15*

12. (   ) Cash Offer. The purchase price amount is available to Buyer and Buyer will provide written proof of funds to Seller within _____ days of Acceptance. _____.

13. Proof of Funds. Buyer agrees to provide written proof of funds to Seller within _____ days from the date of Acceptance. Proof of down payment, and/ or proof of the balance of the purchase price are required.

14. Property Disclosures. Seller represents to Buyer that Seller is unaware of any information that materially affect the value of the Property including violations of governmental laws, rules and regulations, other than those Buyer can observe or that are known or have been disclosed to Buyer. Further, Seller represents that square footage is approximate and Seller does not guarantee accuracy.

Seller declares that Buyer is purchasing the Property upon Buyer's own examination and not by reason of any representation made by Seller, except those that may have been made in this Agreement and in the disclosure statement.

Buyer understands that Seller makes no representations as to the future value of the Property and Seller strongly advises that Buyer verify any and all conditions of the Property and that Buyer should consult their own respective attorncy, accountants, or other professions as to the legal and tax effect of this Agreement prior to signing.

15. Home Warranty Contract. If marked in paragraph 17, a home warranty service contract will be purchased from _____ _____. The Buyer and Seller acknowledge that the home warranty service contract provides limited coverage and may contain specific exclusions and or deductibles. The home warranty company may or may not conduct an inspection of the Property. Any inspection report made available by the provider of the warranty is not meant as a representation of the condition of the Property by the Seller, and is only a report by which the warranty provider uses to determine the conditions under which the Property may be warranted. Seller is not responsible for such home warranty coverage or lack thereof.

16. Inspections and or Surveys. Seller strongly encourages Buyer to employ competent professionals to perform inspections or surveys of all conditions of the Property in order to satisfy any concerns Buyer may have.

(A) If Buyer fails to order an inspection or survey to which Buyer has agreed to pay, then Buyer may not use the failure to receive the document by the delivery deadline as reason to terminate this Agreement.

(B) Objections by Buyer must be provided to Seller in writing along with the inspector's or the surveyor's report by the objection deadline. Buyer may request, in writing, that Seller cure the objection; otherwise Buyer may terminate this Agreement.

(C) If no written objection or termination is received by Seller by the objection deadline, then Buyer will be deemed to have waived the contingency of this Agreement.

(D) Inspection or Survey reports ordered by Seller must be provided to Buyer by delivery deadline. If they are not received by Buyer, Buyer may elect to extend the delivery deadline or terminate this Agreement.

(E) Unless agreed to in writing, the party paying for the inspection or survey will choose the inspection or survey company and will be responsible to order the survey or inspection report. Payment is required for all surveys or inspections performed whether or not the sale of the Property closes.

INSPECTION or SURVEY	BUYER PAYS	SELLER PAYS	DELIVERY DEADLINE	OBJECTION DEADLINE	RESOLUTION DEADLINE
American Land Title Association (ALTA)					
Staked Boundary					
Flood Plain Designation					
Improvement Location Report					
Electrical					
Plumbing					
Heating & Air Conditioning					
Structural					
Roof					
Risk Assessment					
Lead-Based Paint Evaluation					
Radon					
Wood-Destroying Pests					
Dry Rot					
Mold					
Asbestos					
Other:					
Other:					
Other					

Buyer _____ Seller _____

(F) If a resolution of any objections is not resolved by the resolution deadline, then this Agreement will be deemed terminated.

(G) If Seller agrees to cure objections, they must be cured no later than _____ days after the resolution deadline.

(H) Seller agrees to provide Buyer and any inspectors and/or surveyors reasonable access to the Property. The party selecting the inspector will be responsible to pay for any damages that occur to the Property by reason of such inspection or survey.

(I) If Buyer chooses not to have any surveys or inspections, Buyer then waives the right to receive such reports and discharges any claims that may arise due to later findings.

(J) Seller agrees to pay for any repairs required by FHA, VA, a conventional lender, or for repairs under Buyer's objections subject to the maximum cost of: $_____. If the cost exceeds this dollar amount, Buyer and Seller may negotiate a resolution. If no resolution is reached, this Agreement will be deemed terminated.

(K) If this Agreement is terminated subject to the conditions listed in this section titled *Inspections and or Surveys*, the earnest money will be refunded to the Buyer.

17. Costs. Buyer & Seller agree to pay the following items as marked:
B = Buyer   S = Seller   N/A = Not applicable

Loan-Related Charges.

Appraisal Fee (   )   Appraisal Re-inspection Fee (   )
Credit Report (   )   Flood Zone certification (   )
Loan Assumption/Transfer (   )   Origination Fee (   )
Points Buy-down (   )   Points Discount (   )
Tax Service Fee (   )   Underwriting Review Fee (   )
Loan Documentation Preparation (   )
Other (   )
Describe Other: _____

Prepaid Items Required by the Lender.

Hazard Insurance (   )   Flood Insurance (   )
Interest (   )   PMI or MIP (   )
Taxes (   )   Other (   )

Describe Other: _____

Title Company Closing Costs.

Closing Fee (   )   Legal Document Preparation (   )
Special Assessment Search (   )   Transfer Fees (   )
Recording Fees (   )   Other (   )

Describe Other: _____

Policy Premiums.

Title Commitment (   )   Standard Owner's Policy (   )
Mortgagee's Policy (   )   Survey (   )
Impact Fees (   )   Home Warranty Contract (   )
Transfer Fees (   )   Other (   )
Describe Other: _____

Escrow Fees.

Set up   (   )   Periodic   (   )
Close out (   )   Other   (   )
Describe other: _____

18. Prorated Items. Any and all applicable specific fees regarding the Property, including but not limited to rent or lease payments, general real estate taxes, insurance payments, interest, rents and other expenses and revenue of the Property, and homeowners' association dues will be prorated as of the date of closing. Buyer and Seller will directly handle any contract service agreements. Seller will be responsible for disclosing such contract service agreements to the Buyer.

19. Assessments. All assessments, bonds, and impact fees that are part or paid with the Property tax bill of the Property shall be assumed by Buyer. If other assessments, bonds, and impact fees constitute a lien upon the Property, the current installment will be prorated as of the Closing date, and Buyer shall

Buyer _____ Seller _____   *Page 8 of 15*

assume future installments. This Agreement is contingent upon verification and written approval by Buyer and Seller of the amount of all assessments, bonds, and impact fees to be assumed or paid within ten (10) days after receipt of the title commitment approval date. In the event that either party disapproves, such party may terminate this Agreement by giving a written notice to the other party on or before the approval date. Buyer will pay the future assessments for improvements including, but not limited to, sidewalks, driveway cuts or roads.

20. Title and Liens. (   ) Buyer or (   ) Seller will order a title commitment. Such title commitment will be ordered from _____ _____ (title company) within _____ days after acceptance. Buyer will have _____ days (objection deadline) to object to title exceptions after receiving the title commitment and all accompanying documents referred to therein. Unless the Buyer provides written objection to the Seller by the objection deadline, any exceptions to the title will be deemed approved.

If Seller is unwilling or unable to remove such exceptions before the Settlement Signing Date, Seller will provide written notice to Buyer within _____ days after receipt of Buyer's objections. Buyer may choose to close subject to exceptions; remove said exceptions at Buyer's expense; reduce the amount of the purchase price subject to Seller approval; or terminate this Agreement. If Buyer terminates this agreement, the earnest money will be refunded to Buyer.

21. Deed. Conveyance of the Property by _____ subject only to any items identified in the title commitment and not objected to by Buyer as provided in paragraph 20. The legal description written in the deed will be the same legal description written in the title commitment and any survey obtained under paragraph 16.

22. Insurance Contingency. This agreement is contingent upon Buyer being able to obtain, at normal and customary rates, a homeowner's or property insurance binder on the Property. If Buyer fails to make application for insurance within _____ days after date of acceptance of this Agreement, then this contingency will be deemed waived. If Buyer is unable to obtain such a binder for insurance after making a good faith effort and gives timely notice of such inability, then the Purchase Agreement will terminate and the earnest money will be refunded to Buyer.

23. Seller Disclosure. Seller will deliver in writing to Buyer a Seller's Property Disclosure Statement within _____ days after date of acceptance of this Agreement. Buyer in turn must deliver to Seller any and all objections in writing as they pertain to the disclosure statement within _____ days after having received the Seller's Property Disclosure Statement. The deadline to resolve any objections to the disclosure statement is within _____ days of the date Seller receives written objections from Buyer. In the event that a resolution cannot be reached, this Agreement will terminate.

Other documents required from Seller:_____

_____
Deadlines and obligations noted in paragraph 23 will apply to any additional document requirements listed.

24. Lead-Based Paint.
(   ) The dwelling was built BEFORE 1978 and as required by federal law, an addendum providing Seller's Disclosure of Lead-Based Paint and Lead-Based Paint Hazards is attached to this Agreement. Seller cannot legally accept this offer to purchase until Buyer has received and had an opportunity to review this addendum.

(   ) The dwelling was built in or AFTER 1978. Therefore, Seller is not required to make any disclosure of lead-based paint or lead-based paint hazards.

25. ( ) Septic System. The Property includes an on-site liquid waste system; therefore, the transfer of the Property may be subject to state regulations governing on-site liquid waste systems. Septic System Contingency Addendum No. _____ is attached.

26. Closing. This Agreement to Purchase shall be closed and the General Warranty Deed or other deed shall be delivered to Buyer on or before _____ day of _____, 20___. The closing shall take place at the office of _____ (Seller's attorney, Buyer's lender, the Escrow Agent, Title Insurance officer or as otherwise agreed upon).

Unless otherwise agreed in writing, failure to close the sale on the closing date shall constitute a default under this Purchase Agreement. Buyer and Seller agree to sign and deliver to the closing officer all documents required to complete the transaction and to perform all other closing obligations for this Agreement on or before the closing date.

Buyer and Seller agree to provide for the delivery of all required certified funds, if any, using wired or other ready funds acceptable to the title company on or before the closing date. In the event of non-payment, the non-performing party may request the other party in writing to extend the closing date. Acceptance of any new closing date must be presented in writing.

27. Possession. Buyer and Seller agree that Seller will give possession of the Property to Buyer by 5 p.m. on: _____.

28. Condition of Property at time of Possession. Seller agrees to deliver possession of said Property in broom-clean condition, and that all personal property not included in this purchase agreement shall be removed from the Property at Seller's expense before delivery of Property to Buyer. Except for ordinary wear and tear, Seller agrees to deliver Property to Buyer in the same condition as existed on the date of acceptance.

29. Walk-through Prior to Closing. Buyer shall have the right to inspect the Property within two days prior to closing date in order to determine if Property is in the same condition, normal wear and tear excepted, as it was at the time of acceptance.

30. Termite Inspection. Within _____ business days from the date of acceptance of this agreement, the Buyer, at Buyer's expense, has the right to obtain an inspection with a written report from a licensed pest control firm as to the evidence of termite or other wood-boring insect infestation on the Property. If infestation exists Buyer has _____ business days upon receiving such report, either to proceed with the purchase or to cancel this agreement. Such cancellation must be in writing and delivered to the Seller within the time-frame noted.

31. Flood Hazard Zone. If the Property is located in a special flood hazard area, Buyer may be required to pay flood insurance in order to obtain a loan secured by the Property. In this event, Buyer may elect to cancel this agreement without penalty and the earnest money will be refunded to Buyer.

32. Zoning. The Property must be properly zoned for _____ _____
_____use.
No deed restrictions should exist against such use at the time of closing; otherwise, Buyer may choose to terminate this agreement without penalty and the earnest money will be refunded to Buyer. It is Buyer's sole responsibility to adequately verify zoning by contacting the city zoning department or by any other such appropriate means.

33. Entire Agreement. This Purchase Agreement, along with the following addendum(s) and any exhibits referred to in this Purchase Agreement constitute the entire agreement between Buyer and Seller and cannot be amended, changed, or modified in any way except by written agreement of both parties. The Buyer and Seller further understand that this offer, if accepted in writing by Seller and delivered to Buyer, constitutes a legally binding contract.

Addendum No. _____

Addendum No. _____

Lead-Based Paint Addendum No. _____

Septic System Contingency Addendum No. _____

Real Estate Contract Addendum No. _____

Miscellaneous Addendum No. _____

34. Notice. All notices must be in writing and delivered to the parties at the addresses shown on the signature page of this Purchase Agreement. Notices may be made by U.S. registered or certified mail with return receipt requested, hand-delivered, or sent by facsimile.

35. By Law. All terms and conditions of this Agreement will be governed by the laws of the state of _____ and are subject to the practices of good faith and fair dealing. Seller is responsible to provide to Buyer, at Seller's expense, all certificates of inspection, certificates of occupancy, or any such items as required by any local ordinance.

36. Mediation. If a dispute arises between the parties relating to this agreement, the parties agree to submit the dispute to mediation. Buyer and Seller will jointly appoint a mediator and equally share the costs of the mediation. If Buyer and Seller cannot agree upon the appointment of a mediator, or if there is no resolution reached through mediation, Buyer and Seller may enforce their rights and obligations under this agreement in any manner provided by law in the state governing this agreement.

37. Attorney Fees. If litigation is instituted to require either party to perform the stipulations of this agreement, then the prevailing party is entitled to recover all costs incurred, including but not limited to attorney fees and court costs as ordered by the court.

38. Fair Housing. Buyer and Seller understand that the Fair Housing Act prohibits discrimination in the sale or financing of housing on the basis of race, color, age, religion, sexual orientation, gender identity, familial status, spousal affiliation, physical or mental handicap, serious medical condition, national origin or ancestry.

39. Risk of Loss. Risk of loss or damage to the Property by any reason is retained by the Seller until closing. Buyer may choose to extend the date of closing to allow Seller to restore the Property to its previous condition; accept the Property "as is" with Seller assigning the insurance proceeds to Buyer at closing; or terminate this Agreement with all earnest money refunded to Buyer.

40. Earnest Money Dispute. If Buyer fails to perform, all money paid pursuant to this agreement by Buyer shall be retained by Seller as consideration for the execution of this agreement as agreed liquidated damages, and in full settlement of any claims or damages. If Seller fails to perform due to factors beyond Seller's control, all money paid by Buyer pursuant to this agreement will be returned to Buyer on demand; or Buyer will only have the right of specific performance.

41. Foreign Sellers. The Foreign Investment in Real Property Tax Act (FIRPTA) may apply if Seller is a foreign person, foreign corporation or partnership, or nonresident alien, unless the purchase price is less than $300,000 and the Buyer intends to use the Property as the Buyer's residence. FIRPTA may require that the Buyer of real Property withhold 10 percent of the sale price and to deposit that amount with the IRS at the time of closing.

(   ) Seller is subject to FIRPTA
(   ) Seller is not subject to FIRPTA

42. Expiration of Offer. This offer will terminate if not accepted before:

_____ (mo/day), _____ (year),_____ (time), (circle) EST, CDT, MST, PDT in writing to Buyer or Buyer's Agent.

Purchase Agreement Signature Page

TIME IS OF THE ESSENCE OF THIS AGREEMENT.

Buyer

Buyer acknowledges that Buyer has read the entire Purchase Agreement and Buyer understands and accepts the terms specified in this agreement.

_____

Print Buyer(s) Name

_____

Buyer Signature   Date/Time

_____

Buyer Address   E-mail

_____

Buyer Home phone   Business phone   Fax

Seller

Seller agrees to sell the property at the price and terms specified in this agreement.

_____

Print Seller(s) Name

_____

Seller Signature   Date/Time

_____

Seller Address   E-mail

_____

Seller Home phone   Business phone   Fax

*Appendix E. **Page from a Property Disclosure Statement***

Major Appliances and Systems

Indicate Yes No or N/A as to whether the following items are in working order:

_____ Oven and Range	_____ Range Hood
_____ Gas Grill	_____ Refrigerator
_____ Freezer	_____ Dishwasher
_____ Disposal	_____ Microwave Oven
_____ Trash Compactor	_____ Water Heater
_____ Water Purifier	_____ Sump Pump
_____ Toilets	_____ Bathtubs/Showers
_____ Sinks	_____ Hot Tub/Spa/Sauna
_____ Pool & equipment	_____ Central Vacuum
_____ Central Humidifier	_____ Electric Air Filter
_____ Ceiling Fans	_____ Bathroom Vent
_____ Smoke Detectors	_____ Security Systems
_____ Intercom	_____ Solar Systems
_____ Garage Door Opener/Remote	_____ Sprinkler System
_____ Satellite Dish	_____ Landscape lighting
_____ Air Conditioner	_____ Plumbing system
_____ Sewer System	_____ Heating & cooling
_____ Electrical System & Wiring	_____ Windows/skylights

Other_____

Structures:

What year was the house built? _____

Are there any room additions room conversions outbuildings structural modifications or repairs made without required permits or not in compliance with the building codes? _____

Are there any defects or problems with the basement foundations slabs fireplaces or chimneys? If yes explain: _____

Are there any defects or problems with driveways sidewalks patios retaining walks decks or porches? If yes explain: _____

Are there any defects or problems with any steps, stairways or railings? If yes, explain: _____

Disclosure of Information on Lead-Based Paint and/or Lead-Based Paint Hazards
Purchase Agreement Addendum No. _____

It is a violation of Federal law for Seller of real estate to accept an offer from Buyer before all parts of this form are completed in the proper order and signed by both Buyer and Seller.

This disclosure and acknowledgment will be attached to the Purchase Agreement dated _____between:

SELLER(s) _____, and the

BUYER(s) _____, for the

property located at: _____

Legal Description: _____

Lead Warning Statement

Residential dwellings built before 1978 might contain lead-based paint. Lead from paint, paint chips and dust can pose health hazards. Lead exposure is especially harmful to young children and pregnant women and may produce permanent neurological damage, including learning disabilities, reduced intelligence quotient, behavioral problems and impaired memory. Before selling pre-1978 housing, Seller must disclose the presence of lead-based paint and/or lead-based paint hazards in the dwelling. Buyer must also receive a federally approved pamphlet on lead poisoning prevention.

Seller hereby gives Buyer the following disclosure as required by law.

Seller states as follows: (Initial appropriate option).

(   ) Known lead-based paint and/or lead-based paint hazards are present in the housing. Explain _____

(   ) Seller has no knowledge of lead-based paint and/or lead-based paint hazards.

(   ) Seller has provided Buyer with all available records and reports pertaining to lead-based paint and/or lead-based paint hazards in the housing. Documents provided are _____

_____

(   ) Seller has no reports or records pertaining to lead-based paint and/or lead-based paint hazards in the housing.

Buyer's Acknowledgement

(   ) Buyer has received copies of all information listed in the Seller's Requirement section.

(   ) Buyer has received the pamphlet *Protect Your Family From Lead in Your Home.*

Buyer's Rights

(   ) Buyer has received a 10 day opportunity (or a mutually agreed upon time period) to conduct a risk assessment or inspection for the presence of lead-based paint and/or lead-based paint hazards.

(   ) Buyer waives the opportunity to conduct a risk assessment or inspection for the presence of lead-based paint and/or lead-based paint hazards.

Certification of Accuracy

Seller hereby certifies having reviewed this information and that the information Seller provided is true and correct to the best of their knowledge.

_____ | Date _____ | Time _____
Seller Signature

_____ | Date _____ | Time _____
Seller Signature

_____
Seller Name(s) Print

_____
Seller(s) Address   City   State   Zip

_____
Seller Home Phone   Business Phone   Fax

Buyer hereby certifies having reviewed the above information provided by the Seller.

_____ | Date _____ | Time _____
Buyer Signature

_____ | Date _____ | Time _____
Buyer Signature

_____
Buyer Name(s) Print

_____
Buyer(s) Address   City   State   Zip

_____
Buyer Home Phone   Business Phone   Fax

WIN-A-HOUSE RAFFLE AGREEMENT

This agreement is made between the following parties:

_____
(Charity)

and _____.
(Homeowner)

Homeowner Involvement

1. The Charity and the Homeowner agree to the following terms in regards to the Homeowner's involvement in ticket sales and the promotion of the raffle. (Check appropriate option).

(   ) The Homeowner *will not* take an active roll in ticket sales and the promotion of the house raffle.

(   ) The Homeowner *will take* an active roll in ticket sales and the promotion of the house raffle by performing the following tasks: _____

_____

_____

_____

_____

_____

_____

Conclusion of the Raffle

2. Upon the successful conclusion of the house raffle for the prize home located at _____, the Charity will compensate the Homeowner the sum of $_____ DOLLARS for performing the tasks noted in paragraph one (1) of this Agreement. Payment will be made by certified funds prior to the Charity awarding any monies to raffle prize winners.

Initial: Charity _____ Homeowner _____   *Page 1 of 3*

3. By agreeing to accept payment for the performance of the duties noted in paragraph one (1) of this Agreement, the Homeowner assumes no liability for the outcome of the raffle, or the successful sale of the required number of tickets to hold the drawing on the date outlined in the Raffle Rules and Restrictions. Furthermore, at no time will the Homeowner have custody or control of the money received for ticket sales.

4. At the successful conclusion of the house raffle, the Purchase Agreement dated _____ for the prize home is in effect until closing is complete as specified in said Purchase Agreement between the Charity and the Homeowner.

5. Prior to awarding any raffle prizes, the Charity will obtain the required documentation in order to qualify the winners according to the Raffle Rules and Restrictions.

6. Prior to awarding raffle prizes, the Charity is obligated to complete the necessary tax forms for raffle winners and withhold any and all taxes as required by the IRS for such winners. After doing so, the Charity will award the raffle prizes in accordance with the Raffle Rules and Restrictions.

7. In accordance with the Raffle Rules and Restrictions, the Charity will close escrow with the winner of the prize home and pay the Grand Prize winner's closing costs. In the event that the Grand Prize winner chooses the cash prize, the Charity will award the alternate cash prize as outlined in the Raffle Rules and Restrictions.

8. In the event that the Grand Prize winner is awarded the alternate cash prize, one of the following will take effect: (Check appropriate option).

(   ) The Charity will retain title to the prize home and may, at its discretion, sell the property.

(   ) The Holding Fee Agreement between the Homeowner and the Charity will apply as outlined in Addendum No. _____ to the Real Estate Purchase Agreement dated _____ for the prize home.

9. In the event the house raffle is canceled due to insufficient raffle ticket sales, the Purchase Agreement dated _____ for the prize home will be deemed terminated and the Charity will return the money received for raffle ticket sales to ticket purchasers in accordance with the Raffle Rules and Restrictions. Furthermore, the Charity will no longer be obligated to compensate the Homeowner for tasks noted in paragraph one (1) of this Agreement unless alternate arrangements to the contrary have been agreed upon in writing by both parties. See Alternate Agreement No._____ .

Acceptance of Agreement

Charity and Homeowner understand and accept the terms specified on this agreement.

_____
Print Name & Title of person with legal authority to sign for the Charity

_____
Signature   Date

_____
Print Name of Homeowner

_____
Signature   Date

_____
Signature   Date

Sign me up for the Win-a-House Raffle
*in support of*_____

---

*(Name of Charity)*_____ *is a 501c ( ) tax exempt organization.*

Your ticket confirmation will be sent after payment has been verified; the official ticket is placed in the drawing container. You must be 18 years of age and have a valid Social Security number to purchase a ticket. (Proof required upon claiming prize)

Name _____

Mailing Address _____

City _____State _____ Zip _____

Home phone _____Cell phone _____

E-Mail _____

I want to purchase _____ tickets at $_____ each. Total included: $_____

I am paying by ( ) Cash ( )Check ( )Money Order ( )VISA
( ) MasterCard ( )Discover ( )American Express

Make checks payable to _____

Credit Card # _____
CVV Code (3 digits on back) _____ Expiration: Month _____ Year _____
Zip code your bill goes to _____
Full Name on the card _____
Signature _____

FAX or Mail with Payment to: _____
LAST DAY TO _____
MAIL_____ _____

I have received the Rules & Restrictions:	Ticket Number(s) FOR TICKET SELLER ONLY
Signature _____	

*Appendix I. **Entry Form With a Credit Card Machine***

Sign me up for the Win-a-House Raffle
in support of _____

(Name of Charity)   *is a 501c ( ) tax exempt organization.*

Your ticket confirmation will be sent after payment has been verified; the official ticket is placed in the drawing container. You must be 18 years of age and have a valid Social Security number to purchase a ticket. (Proof required upon claiming prize)

Name _____

Mailing Address _____

City _____ State _____ Zip _____

Home phone _____ Cell phone _____

E-Mail _____

I want to purchase _____ tickets at $_____ each. Total included: $_____

I am paying by ( ) Cash   ( )Check   ( )Money Order   ( )VISA
             ( ) MasterCard ( )Discover ( )American Express

Make checks payable to _____

FAX or Mail with Payment to: _____
                              _____
                              _____

LAST DAY TO MAIL: _____

I have received the Rules & Restrictions:	Ticket Number(s) FOR TICKET SELLER ONLY
Signature _____	

Appendix J. *Ticket Sales Log Sheet*

TICKET NO.	DATE SOLD	(BUYER) FIRST NAME	(BUYER) LAST NAME	PAYMENT TYPE

WIN A HOUSE
or
(Charity Logo)
$100,000.00 CASH!

*Raffle Benefiting*_____.

Only 4,000 tickets will be sold!! Only $100/ticket
Drawing is _____

```
+-----------------------------------------------+
|                                               |
|           Picture of the prize home           |
|                                               |
|                                               |
+-----------------------------------------------+
```

Three Ways to Buy:

- Purchase tickets on line at www_____
- Buy tickets in person at the following locations: _____

  _____
- Buy tickets by completing the Entry Form on the back of this flier, and fax or mail it in. Deadline to mail is _____

For additional information: (000) 000-0000
www._____

WIN A 4 BEDROOM HOME
or
$100,000.00 CASH!
Raffle Benefiting

For less than the cost of 27 cups of your morning grande-soy-latte-frappe-coffee, you could own a beautiful 4 bedroom home on 1/2 acre with mountain views or $100,000.00 cash.

OPEN HOUSE
Sunday
11 a.m. – 6 p.m.
ONLY 4,000 Raffle Tickets will be sold!
$100/ticket

---

714 Silver Drive
Three blocks east of Champion State Park

(Directions: _____)

_____ *is a 501(c)_ tax-exempt organization.*

For More Information
Call: (000) 000-0000
www._____

Charity
Logo

CERTIFICATE
OF WINNING

Congratulations!

_____

Name of Winner

Your ticket # _____has been drawn as the winning number

for the _____ prize of the

Win-A-House Raffle benefiting:

_____

Thank you for your participation in the raffle, and we join you in your excitement over winning this great prize. In order to claim your prize, please follow the enclosed Instructions.

_____

(Name of Charity)

is a 501(c)__ non-profit organization organized under the laws
of the state of _____

Note: Winner must meet all requirements stated in the Raffle Rules and Restrictions. If the winner is disqualified, the next ticket drawn will be assigned as the winner for this prize.

(Charity name, address, telephone number, website)

WIN-A-HOUSE RAFFLE
<u>Winner Instruction Sheet</u>

Follow these instructions to claim your prize.

1. Call _____ the House Raffle Coordinator at
_____ to make an appointment to meet.
(Phone Number)

You must claim the prize in person by 5.00 p.m. _____ (within 30 days of the drawing date) or make alternative arrangements acceptable to the House Raffle Coordinator in order to claim the prize on or before the deadline.

2. The meeting to claim the prize will be at the agreed upon time at the prize home located at _____
_____

3. Bring the following items to the meeting:

- Two proofs of identification such as your driver's license, passport, Social Security Card, Voter's Registration or Military ID Card. Copies are not acceptable.

- Proof of Social Security number such as a Social Security Card or Voter's Registration.

4. If you are the Grand Prize winner, please consider the two prize options – the house or the cash. The current fair market value of the home is $_____. At the meeting you will be asked to provide written proof of your decision as to which prize you will accept.

(Charity name, address, telephone number, website)

Win-a-House Raffle

Benefiting_____

<u>Winner Affidavit of Eligibility</u>

The owner of the winning ticket number _____

is _____ .

The above named prize winner hereby declares the following by initialing each item.

_____ I hereby declare that I am not a Board member, agent, or employee of _____ ,

(Name of Charity)

_____ I hereby declare that I am not a Board member, agent, or employee of_____ .

(Homeowner)

_____ I hereby declare that I am not an immediate family member of the Charity or the Homeowner noted on this affidavit.

_____ I hereby declare that I have received a copy of the Rules and Restrictions of the raffle, and understand that acceptance of the prize constitutes acceptance of the Rules and Restrictions of said raffle.

_____
Signature of Winner   Date

Page 1 of 2

LIST DOCUMENTS PROVIDED TO VERIFY PROOF OF IDENTITY

_____

_____

LIST DOCUMENTS PROVIDED TO VERIFY PROOF OF SOCIAL
SECURITY NUMBER _____

_____

Received by:

_____
(Print name of charity representative accepting documents noted)

_____
(Signature of charity representative accepting documents noted)

_____ Initial of charity representative indicates that copies of all original
substantiating documents are attached.

(Charity name, address, telephone number, website)

Purchase Agreement Addendum <u>No A</u>.
"House Raffle Withholding"

The following agreement is an addendum to the Purchase Agreement dated
_____between the

Seller _____, and the

(Print name of Charity)

Buyer _____, for

(Print name of Grand Prize Winner)

the property located at: _____

_____

(Address of Prize Home)

Legal Description: _____

_____.

This purchase agreement is contingent on the Buyer providing _____%
the tax withholding amount for winning a prize with a fair market value of
$_____ less $_____

(cost of raffle ticket)

Total amount required from Buyer is $_____.

Buyer agrees to deliver certified funds using wired or other ready funds
acceptable to the settlement company on or before the closing date of
_____.

_____

Buyer Signature   Date

_____

Seller Signature   (Person legally authorized to sign for Charity   Date

Department of the Treasury

Internal Revenue Service
www.irs.gov
Notice 1340
(March 2005)

Tax-Exempt Organizations and Raffle Prizes
Reporting Requirements and Federal Income Tax Withholding

Tax-Exempt and Government Entities Division
Tax-Exempt Organizations and Raffle Prizes
Reporting Requirements and Federal Income Tax Withholding
Tax-Exempt and Government Entities Division

This notice discusses federal tax reporting and income tax withholding requirements that apply to raffles conducted by organizations exempt under section 501 of the Internal Revenue Code. A tax-exempt organization that sponsors raffles may be required to secure information about the winner(s) and file reports on the prizes with the Internal Revenue Service. The organization may also be required to withhold and remit federal income taxes on prizes.

Reporting Raffle Prizes
"Raffle" Defined: In general, a raffle is considered a form of lottery. As such, a raffle generally refers to a method for the distribution of prizes among persons who have paid for a chance to win such prizes, usually determined by the numbers, or symbols, on tickets drawn.

Generally, an exempt organization must report raffle prizes if (a) the amount paid reduced, at the exempt organization's option, by the wager (the amount a person paid for the chance to win a prize), is $600 or more; and (b) the payout is at least 300 times the amount of the wager. The organization uses Form W-2G for this report.

Example 1: Wendy purchased a $1 ticket for a raffle conducted by X, an exempt organization. On October 31, 2004, the drawing was held and Wendy won $900. X must file Form W-2G with the IRS and give a copy of Form W-2G to Wendy.

A person receiving gambling winnings must furnish the exempt organization a statement on Form 5754 made under penalties of perjury stating his or her identity and the identity of any others entitled to the winnings (and their shares of the winnings.) When the person receiving winnings is not the actual winner, or is a member of a group of two or more winners on a single ticket, the recipient must furnish the exempt organization information listed on Form 5754, *Statement by Person(s) Receiving Gambling Winnings*, and the organization must file Forms W-2G based on that information. The organization must keep Form 5754 for four years and make it available for IRS inspection. (See the specific instructions for Form 5754 for more information.)

The exempt organization must file Forms W-2G with the IRS by the last day of February of the year after the year of the raffle. Use Form 1096, *Annual Summary and Transmittal of U.S. Information Returns*, to transmit Forms W-2G to the IRS. The organization must also issue Forms W-2G to prize recipients by January 31 of the year after the year of the raffle.

Withholding Tax on Raffle Prizes
Regular Gambling Withholding: An organization that pays raffle prizes must withhold 25% from the winnings and report this amount to the IRS on Form W-2G. This *regular gambling withholding* applies to winnings of more than $5,000. If the organization fails to withhold correctly, it is liable for the tax.

Example 2: Lou purchased a $1 ticket for a raffle conducted by X, an exempt organization. On October 31, 2004, the drawing was held and Lou won $6,000. Because the proceeds from the wager are greater than $5,000 ($6,000 prize minus $1 ticket cost), X must withhold $1,499.75 ($5,999 x 25%) from Lou's winnings. If X fails to withhold $1,499.75 before distributing the prize, X is liable for the withholding tax.
Catalog Number 39810E

Backup Withholding: An organization is required to withhold 28 percent of the total proceeds if (1) the prize is otherwise subject to reporting (i.e., the amount of the prize, less the amount wagered, is $600 or more and 300 times the amount of the wager), *and* (2) the winner fails to furnish a correct taxpayer identification number (social security number, individual taxpayer identification number, or employer identification number). This is called backup withholding.

Noncash Prizes: For noncash prizes, the winner must pay the organization 25% of the fair market value of the prize minus the amount of the wager.

Example 3: Jason purchased a $1 ticket for a raffle conducted by X, an exempt organization. On October 31, 2004, the drawing was held and Jason won a car worth

$10,000 (fair market value). Because the prize exceeds $5,000 and the fair market value of the car is $10,000, the tax on the fair market value of the prize is $2,499.75 [($10,000 minus $1 ticket cost) x 25%)]. Jason must pay $2,499.75 to X to remit to the IRS on his (Jason's) behalf. X would indicate the fair market value of the prize ($10,000) in box 1 and the amount of the withholding tax paid ($2,499.75) in box 2 on Form W-2G.

Organization Pays Withholding Tax: If the organization, as part of the prize, pays the taxes required to be withheld, it must pay tax not only on the fair market value of the prize less the wager, but also on the taxes it pays on behalf of the winner. This results in a *grossed up* prize requiring the use of an algebraic formula. Under this formula, the organization must pay withholding tax of 33.33% of the prize's fair market value. The organization reports the *grossed up* amount of the prize (fair market value of prize plus amount of taxes paid on behalf of winner) in box 1 of Form W-2G, and the withholding tax in box 2 of Form W-2G.

Example 4: If in Example 3, X pays the withholding tax on Jason's behalf, the withholding tax is $3,332.67 [($10,000 fair market value of prize minus $1 ticket cost) x 33.33%]. X must report $13,333 as the gross winnings in box 1 of Form W-2G, and $3,334.67 withholding tax in box 2.

Reporting and Paying Tax to the IRS
The organization must use Form 945, *Annual Return of Withheld Federal Income Tax*, to report and send withheld amounts to the IRS. This is NOT the same form used to report Federal income tax withheld and FICA with respect to employees. Form 945 is an annual return, and is due January 31 of the year after the year in which the taxes were withheld (for example, for taxes withheld in 2004, the return would be due January 31, 2005). Separate tax deposits are required for payroll and non-payroll withholding. Be sure to mark the Form 945 checkbox on Form 8109, the Federal tax deposit coupon.

The organization must list the EIN (employer identification number) of the organization conducting the raffle on Forms W-2G, 1096, and 945. If you have not secured an EIN, you may apply for one on Form SS-4, *Application for Employer Identification Number*, available from the IRS. You may also apply for an EIN on-line at www.irs.gov , under the topic Employer ID Numbers on the *Businesses* Contents page.

For more information, see IRS Publication 3079, *Gaming Publication for Tax-Exempt Organizations*, or call EO Customer Account Services at 1-877-829-5500 (toll-free). IRS forms and publications can be ordered by calling toll-free
1-800-TAX-FORM (1-800-8293676) or from the IRS Web site (www.irs.gov)

Win-a-House Raffle

Benefiting_____
(Name of Charity)

Grand Prize Acceptance Statement

I hereby choose to accept _____
(Raffle Home or Cash)

as my grand prize.

_____
Print Name of Grand Prize winner

_____
Signature of Grand Prize winner   Date/Time

Received by:

_____
Print name of Charity representative & title

_____
Signature of Charity representative   Date/Time

(Charity name, address, telephone number, website)

RESOURCES

Books

Dress Your House For Success: 5 fast, easy steps to selling your house, apartment, or condo for the highest possible price
    by Martha Webb and Sarah Parsons Zackheim

This Sold House: Staging Your Home To Sell in Today's Market
    by Diane Keyes

301 Simple Things You Can Do to Sell Your Home Now and For More Money Than You Thought
    by Teri B. Clark

Home Staging For Dummies
    by Christine Rae and Janice Saunders Maresh

Nonprofit Internet Strategies: Best Practices for Marketing, Communications, and Fundraising Success
    by Ted Hart, James M. Greenfield and Michael Johnston

The New Rules of Marketing and PR: How to Use Social Media, Blogs, News Releases, Online Video, and Viral Marketing to Reach Buyers Directly, 2nd Edition
    by David Meerman Scott

Robin Hood Marketing: Stealing Corporate Savvy to Sell Just Causes
    by Katya Andresen

Online Sites

Free and low cost Real Estate Forms
www.kaktus.com

State specific real estate forms
www.uslegalforms.com

Information on raffle laws for each state
www.rafflefaq.com/united-states-raffle-laws

IRS Gaming Publication for Tax-Exempt Organizations
www.irs.gov/pub/irs-pdf/p3079.pdf

IRS notice for Tax-Exempt Organizations and Raffle Prizes – Reporting
Requirements and Federal Income Tax Withholding
www.irs.gov/pub/irs-tege/notice_1340.pdf

Charity ratings on Charity Navigator: Your Guide to Intelligent Giving
www.charitynavigator.org

Leading consultants to nonprofit organizations
www.givinginstitute.org

Information on nonprofit organizations
www.guidestar.org

The newspaper of the nonprofit world
www.philanthropy.com

Outdoor Advertising Company Directory
www.outdoorbillboard.com

ACKNOWLEDGEMENTS

To my sister Angelina Giraudo, and to my friends, Joyce Crettol, and Esther Pringle—your encouragement during the writing of this book and your help with raffle ticket sales and distributing fliers was phenomenal. Ron Thomas, thank you for tirelessly placing 40 Open House signs on many Sundays; I could not have done it without you. Nancy Anderson—a special thank you for your friendship, your wise advice, and for encouraging me to write a book proposal for this book. A great big thank you to Joyce Crettol and Diane Devitto, for your editing work on the manuscript—you helped to make this a better book. Lastly, thank you to the entire team at Morgan James Publishing for believing in my project and taking a chance on a new author.

Diane Giraudo McDermott

ABOUT THE AUTHOR

Diane Giraudo McDermott is a native of Albuquerque, New Mexico. She graduated from the University of New Mexico with a Bachelor of Science degree in Education. After teaching in the public schools for several years in New Mexico and California, she moved into sales and marketing—focusing on print media advertising. In 1983 she purchased her first piece of real estate in California.

Currently, Diane is president and owner of DGM Solutions, Inc., a real estate investment company that purchases foreclosure and tax auction properties to hold or remodel and re-sell. She owns real estate in New Mexico, California, and Oregon. Diane is a member of two real estate groups, Invest in Debt and ABQ Congress on Real Estate (ACRE). The primary focus of these groups is to provide solid knowledgeable education and networking for real estate investors.

Throughout her life, Diane has always been a creative problem solver and an advocate of animal rights. In 2009, she organized and managed the sale of a house through a raffle benefiting a no-kill animal shelter and she has since consulted on several house raffles. She also offers workshops for homeowners, real estate agents, and fundraising directors of nonprofit organizations on the subject of house raffles. Diane's personal goal is to continuously support America's no-kill animal shelters—"Domesticated animals are innocent and completely subject to the choices man has made for them. I see them as a wonderful expression of an idea that started in the mind of God. I believe we owe them compassionate care."

For information on consulting, workshops, teleclasses, and the latest information and resources regarding house raffles, please visit the author's website at: www.isoldmyhouseinaraffle.com

To download FREE full-size copies of the sample forms provided in the Appendices, visit www.isoldmyhouseinaraffle.com/appendices-download

(Please note that there are inherent risks involved in holding a house raffle; therefore, prior to using the samples in the Appendices, the user is strongly advised to take the time to gain full knowledge and understanding of the information outlined in this book and to consult experts in the specific field in order to be sure that the sample forms meet local and state laws and ordinances).

BUY A SHARE OF THE FUTURE IN YOUR COMMUNITY

These certificates make great holiday, graduation and birthday gifts that can be personalized with the recipient's name. The cost of one S.H.A.R.E. or one square foot is $54.17. The personalized certificate is suitable for framing and will state the number of shares purchased and the amount of each share, as well as the recipient's name. The home that you participate in "building" will last for many years and will continue to grow in value.

Here is a sample SHARE certificate:

HABITAT FOR HUMANITY

THIS CERTIFIES THAT

YOUR NAME HERE

HAS INVESTED IN A HOME FOR A DESERVING FAMILY

1985-2005

TWENTY YEARS OF BUILDING FUTURES IN OUR
COMMUNITY ONE HOME AT A TIME

1200 SQUARE FOOT HOUSE @ $65,000 = $54.17 PER SQUARE FOOT
This certificate represents a tax deductible donation. It has no cash value.

YES, I WOULD LIKE TO HELP!

I support the work that Habitat for Humanity does and I want to be part of the excitement! As a donor, I will receive periodic updates on your construction activities but, more importantly, I know my gift will help a family in our community realize the dream of homeownership. **I would like to SHARE in your efforts against substandard housing in my community!** *(Please print below)*

PLEASE SEND ME _____ SHARES at $54.17 EACH = $ $_____

In Honor Of: _____

Occasion: (Circle One) HOLIDAY BIRTHDAY ANNIVERSARY

OTHER: _____

Address of Recipient: _____

Gift From: _____ *Donor Address:* _____

Donor Email: _____

I AM ENCLOSING A CHECK FOR $ $_____ PAYABLE TO HABITAT FOR HUMANITY OR PLEASE CHARGE MY VISA OR MASTERCARD *(CIRCLE ONE)*

Card Number _____ Expiration Date: _____

Name as it appears on Credit Card _____ Charge Amount $ _____

Signature _____

Billing Address _____

Telephone # Day _____ Eve _____

PLEASE NOTE: Your contribution is tax-deductible to the fullest extent allowed by law.
Habitat for Humanity • P.O. Box 1443 • Newport News, VA 23601 • 757-596-5553
www.HelpHabitatforHumanity.org

9 781600 377310